T0315022

JOSSEY-BASS
A Wiley Brand

Stewardship Essentials

The Donor Relations Guide

Scott C. Stevenson, Editor

WILEY

978-1-118-69040-6   ISBN

978-1-118-70418-9   ISBN (online)

Stewardship Essentials
The Donor Relations Guide

Published by

Stevenson, Inc.

P.O. Box 4528 • Sioux City, Iowa • 51104
Phone 712.239.3010 • Fax 712.239.2166
www.stevensoninc.com

TABLE OF CONTENTS

Stewardship Essentials: The Donor Relations Guide

TABLE OF CONTENTS

Stewardship Essentials: The Donor Relations Guide

STEWARDSHIP MANAGEMENT AND TRACKING PROCEDURES

Though it's likely many people will be involved in stewarding those who have generously invested in your charity, one person should be responsible for the overall management of your stewardship program. Those organizations that have a long history of gift support have systems, policies and procedures in place. This chapter addresses some of those key issues.

Key Stewardship Relations Practices

Each profession has unique customer relations principles. To excel in the fundraising profession, adhere to these practical tips for maintaining good stewardship practices:

- Acknowledge all gifts within 48 hours in as personalized way as possible.
- Send letters to prospects confirming appointment times and the purpose of the visit.
- Follow up visits with a letter summarizing key points and confirming next steps.
- Show that donors' gifts are being used as intended through progress reports, tours, etc.
- Confirm how a donor wishes to have his/her name listed in your annual report.

- Thank a donor seven times — in different ways — before asking for another gift.
- Include both spouses in the solicitation process (unless directed otherwise).
- Avoid doing end runs to get to the top decision-maker. Follow protocol.
- Be up-front about the time required for an appointment and then stick to it.
- If you are unable to answer an individual's question with confidence, assure him/her you will get the answer, and then make a point to follow up within 48 hours.
- When a donor or prospective donor takes the time to stop by your office — even without an appointment — make every effort to meet with him/her.

Regularly Test Your Stewardship Practices

How does your organization score when it comes to stewarding existing donors? To find out, ask your contributors.

Once every three years, conduct a random survey of existing donors and ask to be rated on the following points:

- Type of gift acknowledgment received.
- Timeliness of thank yous.
- Who does the thanking.
- Frequency of donor recognition.

- Understanding of how gifts are making a positive difference.

Donors' responses will help to pinpoint positive practices as well as those that need more attention. Plus, the surveys will accomplish two additional objectives: 1) Cultivation toward future gifts will occur as a result of seeking these individuals' advice; and 2) you will be demonstrating that you really do care about the ways in which you show appreciation and recognize generosity.

Organizations Need to Be Careful Stewards

What steps do you take to inform donors how their gifts have been used?

Donors need to be assured that their gifts will be used for the purposes for which they were given or many of the donors may become disenchanted with your organization and stop making gifts, says John Taylor, associate vice chancellor for advancement services at North Carolina State University (Raleigh, NC).

"Many donors think that organizations don't spend donated funds in the manner for which they were intended," he says.

This perception, says Taylor, goes back to how donors are being informed about how their gifts are being used. This is exacerbated by the fact that donors are hearing in the news that organizations are misusing donors' funds.

"This could easily be fixed by communicating to donors during the course of the expenditure of the funds how those funds are being used," he says.

Source: John Taylor, Associate Vice Chancellor for Advancement Services, North Carolina State University, Raleigh, NC. Phone (919) 513-2954. E-mail: johntaylor@ncsu.edu

STEWARDSHIP MANAGEMENT AND TRACKING PROCEDURES

A Simple Spreadsheet Can Boost Donor Relations

When Angela Townsend became development director at Tabby's Place (Ringoes, NJ) in mid-2008, she quickly realized one of her most important tasks would be to reach out to each donor — large or small — because all are important to the small nonprofit.

"Our donors kind of expect that," Townsend says of the regular recognition. "It's like expecting personal service from a small mom-and-pop shop."

As the organization's sole development staff person, Townsend looked to organize and streamline these outreach efforts to make them more effective.

Using Microsoft Excel, she created a simple but specific spreadsheet that allows her to keep meticulous track of every form of contact with each donor.

The form, Townsend says, "is extremely simple ... and it has become what sets us apart from other organizations."

The development director's spreadsheet consists of five columns that contain:

1. The name of any donor who has made a one-time donation of $100 or more, as well as every regular monthly donor.
2. Space for Townsend to make personal notes to help jog her memory about the donor.
3. Phone numbers for the donor.
4. The date of the last contact Townsend or one of her volunteers had with that donor.
5. Information on what that contact was (e.g., phone call, in-person visit, mailed card).

By sorting the list by the dates in the fourth column, Townsend can easily see who's gone the longest without a contact.

"We try not to let anybody go more than three months without a contact from us," she says, "like a card with photos, a thoughtful note or just a hello and an open call to invite them to come in and see what's going on and what's new." While Townsend was originally handling all of these donor relations by herself, she now regularly uses two volunteers to help write notes and make calls.

The success has been tangible, Townsend says. "Very frequently after one of these outreaches, we get a nice check from one of these folks. And about 20 of our donors have commented specifically that this affection and attention is unlike anything they've ever experienced with any nonprofit before."

Source: Angela Townsend, Director of Development, Tabby's Place, Ringoes, NJ. Phone (908) 237-5300. E-mail: info@tabbysplace.org

This sample Microsoft Excel document illustrates the simple-yet-effective way Angela Townsend, director of development at Tabby's Place (Ringoes, NJ), manages donor contacts.

Content not available in this edition

Are You Working to Build Donor Loyalty?

External forces and distractions pulling at your donors can cause them to decrease, even stop, giving. Counter that by building loyalty, especially among major donors. Part of your operational plan should focus on building loyalty around these examples:

✓ **Look for new ways to recognize donors.** Publicly recognize donors in both small and big ways: feature stories, lists of names, citing personal and professional achievements, creating special awards, VIP treatment at events and more.

✓ **Communicate regularly and often.** Use broad-based and individualized approaches to stay in touch with donors: newsletters, receptions, one-on-one meetings, surveys.

✓ **Build exclusivity among donors.** Provide perks and privileges to those who give at certain levels: induction ceremonies, invitation-only events, insider updates and more.

Craft a Gift Agreement Spelling Out Donor's Wishes

A gift agreement that addresses the interests of both the donor and the charity will provide lasting clarity to both and pave the way for possible additional major gift commitments.

Some gift agreements — often referred to as letters of intent — are designed to spell out the terms of a major gift. In doing so, they often benefit the charity more than the donor. Such gift agreements typically identify key points such as:

- Total pledge amount.
- Pledge payout period — how often gifts will be made and for how much.
- Timing of payments — when they are to be made.
- Intended use of the gift.
- Gift type — cash, equities, land, etc.

As vital as a letter of intent is when accepting a major gift pledge, it is equally important — for the donor's sake — to develop a gift agreement that takes the donor's wishes into account, as well. Whether in the letter of intent or part of a separate document, it's important that certain issues be addressed for the sake of the donor.

While it's true that such a document helps protect the charity as well as the donor, it's simply good stewardship to look out for the best interests of the donor.

This particular example addresses issues such as:

- What is the donor's purpose in making the gift? What specifically does he/she want it to accomplish?
- How much publicity does donor want? Or does he/she want total anonymity?
- Does donor have special conditions attached to the gift? Some donors, for instance, insist on a provision in the event the charity dissolves.

MEADOWLAWN ACADEMY
Major Gift Agreement

To assure that Meadowlawn Academy honors the donor's intent, the following items should be discussed and the form signed by both the donor and the development officer representing the academy.

I. Purpose of gift _____

_____

II. Full name(s) of the donor(s) as they wish to be acknowledged:

_____

III. Does the donor wish to remain anonymous?   ❏ Yes ❏ No

IV. Please check the type of written recognition you would like to receive:

___ Listing in the Annual Report according to giving club levels.

___ Publication of size of gift in internal Academy newsletters

___ Publication of the type of gift in internal newsletters

___ Recognition of the gift in Meadowlawn Academy Magazine

___ Public announcement of the gift to the media

___ No written recognition of any kind

___ Other _____

V. Gift vehicle _____

_____

VI. Gift Amount _____

_____

VII. Any special conditions to this gift _____

_____

VIII. Closing Date _____

Donor _____ Donor _____

Meadowlawn Academy Development Officer _____

Cc: Meadowlawn Academy Marketing
    Meadowlawn Academy Business Office
    Donor's Financial Advisor

This sample gift agreement shows how such a form can emphasize a donor's wishes and take the charity's issues into consideration.

Gift Agreements Good Way to Prevent Donor Disengagement

Gift agreements not only help your organization plan for major gifts, they can be very helpful in preventing donor disengagement, says John Taylor, associate vice chancellor for advancement services, North Carolina State University (Raleigh, NC).

A gift agreement is a legal document that defines certain functions and responsibilities on the part of both the donor and the organization, Taylor says. "If you document everything that is required on behalf of both parties regarding a gift, you run less of a risk of losing the donor because you failed to honor those activities."

By carefully documenting everyone's role, you also run less of a risk of going to court, he says: "We are seeing more lawsuits related to a donor's disagreements with an institution over a gift."

There is no rule of thumb for when a gift agreement is necessary, says Taylor, but they can certainly be helpful in the areas of endowments, scholarships and other major gifts. "A gift agreement is being required more and more based on the dollar amount of the gift," he says.

Gift agreement language should be clear so it can serve as the understanding of a gift now and in the future, says Taylor: "You want the terms to be understood not only by the parties currently involved in the gift agreement, but by those who may have to service the gift agreement in the future. It should also ensure the irrevocability of the gift."

Most gift agreements are two pages or less, and include these basic components, says Taylor:

- Title.
- Introduction.
- Charitable tax information.
- Description of the gift.
- Purpose of the gift.
- Future considerations.
- Recognition and reporting.
- Miscellaneous items such as amendments and the date.
- Signatures.
- Additional information initiated by the donor.

"You should have a standard template for your gift agreement where you basically fill in the blanks and only if the donor wishes to deviate from those standard requirements would you involve an attorney," he says.

Source: John Taylor, Associate Vice Chancellor for Advancement Services, North Carolina State University, Raleigh, NC. (919) 513-2954. E-mail: johnhtaylor@ncsu.edu

How to Reengage Disenchanted Donors

The best way to reengage disenchanted donors is to find out why they went away, apologize for whatever it was and then provide reassurances that you've taken action to fix the problem, says John Taylor, associate vice chancellor for advancement services, North Carolina State University (Raleigh, NC).

"More often than not, the donor is going to tell you what disenchanted them," he says. "It's either going to be something you didn't do and should have done, or something you did do and shouldn't have done. When a donor tells you, make sure they understand that you understand what they've said by mirroring it back to them."

A donor doesn't care why or how it happened, says Taylor, he/she just wants to know that you have taken personal responsibility for it, that you are truly sorry that you created the circumstance for this situation that caused him/her to be upset.

"Don't worry about pointing fingers," Taylor says. "Simply accept blame, even if it was not your fault."

Once you are away from the donor, it's very important that you write down what you have mirrored back to him or her, he says, so that you can accurately fix the problem.

"Follow up with the donor after you have (hopefully) had a satisfactory conversation," says Taylor. "This puts them in the driver's seat."

Steward Donors Year-round

Does your brand-new, $20 donor expect a thank-you call from your CEO?

That's what Christina Thrun, development and marketing director, Big Brothers Big Sisters Northwestern Wisconsin (Eau Claire, WI), wants to know.

You see, her donors don't expect it either — but they get it, thanks to stewardship efforts that have reached a whole new level for the organization.

"Stewardship is more than a thank-you card," she says. "It's everything that you do (throughout the year) that goes above and beyond what the donor expects."

She shares other stewardship steps from the organization's development plan:

✓ Any new donor, no matter how much they give, receives a personal thank-you call from the CEO. New significant donors are offered a meeting with organization staff, at their own office, to hear about the direct impact their gift is making.

✓ Donors receive hand-made cards from the organization's matches (adult volunteers, or "bigs," and their assigned young clients, or "littles"). Staff provides examples of what to write so the donors receive cards that are actually suitable for the intended purpose. The bigs and littles are asked to work on these cards at quarterly big/little events.

✓ Starting in January 2010, donors received thank-you calls from bigs and littles during a phone thank-a-thon tied to National Mentoring Month. Matches were asked to donate 90 minutes of their time, visiting the organization's offices to make calls. Scripts, pizza and soda were provided.

Source: Christina Thrun, Development and Marketing Director, Big Brothers Big Sisters Northwestern Wisconsin, Eau Claire, WI. Phone (715) 835-0161. E-mail: Christina.Thrun@bbbs.org

Use Cumulative Giving as a Cultivation/Stewardship Tool

Do you have records that allow you to determine how much individual donors have given since their first gift? If so, you can take advantage of this information to steward donors and to cultivate future and increased gifts.

Here are a few examples of how to use this information:

Personalize direct mail appeals by incorporating cumulative giving: "Susan, since becoming a member of the Art Center in 1989, you have contributed $5,675 toward enhancing programs and expanding our ability to host exhibits. As a veteran investor in this cause...."

Establish a special society and/or host a special reception for those reaching a cumulative milestone: "All individuals/businesses who contribute $25,000 or more during their lifetimes — including those who make irrevocable planned gifts amounting to $25,000 or more — will be inducted into The Franklin Society and be afforded all the rights and privileges of this elite group."

Send a onetime itemized breakdown of cumulative giving: Once an individual's cumulative giving reaches a particular level, send a onetime summary of gifts by year and the use of each gift. Accompany it with a letter from your CEO or board chair that states: "As you can see by the enclosed summary, we take your many years of generous support very seriously. That's why we hope we continue to merit your support and your thoughtfulness in considering a planned gift to our institution."

If you have not kept a record of cumulative gifts, it's not too late to begin.

Stewardship Essentials: The Donor Relations Guide

GIFT ACKNOWLEDGMENT PROCEDURES

One of the most important rules in fundraising is to acknowledge all gifts within five business days. Anything longer may cast a negative light on your organization. Proper gift acknowledgment is an important first step in the stewardship process. Who expresses thanks, when and the ways in which it is expressed all comprise the acknowledgment procedure. Where does your organization's CEO fit into gift acknowledgment? When is a phone call more appropriate than a letter?

Develop Process for Sending Acknowledgment Letters

Establish a formal system to officially acknowledge major gifts in a timely manner.

At Queen's University (Kingston, Ontario, Canada), all gifts and new pledges of $100,000 or greater are acknowledged with a letter from the principal (the equivalent of the university president), says Karen Logan, stewardship officer.

Logan receives an electronic monthly report from the gift services office on all gifts $100,000 or more. In the week after receiving the report, she drafts the letters (based on a pre-approved template) and sends them to the appropriate relationship managers (the equivalent of development officers) for review and personalization, if needed.

"Although I review contact reports and gift records to gain a basic understanding of the donor and the gift, I also work with whoever helped solicit the gift," she says. "They often know the specific details or some anecdote from the meeting that will make the letter more meaningful."

Letters go to the principal's office for printing on letterhead, signature and mailing.

All key players understand that completing and sending the letters in a timely fashion is in everyone's best interest, the stewardship officer says: "We've created an expectation that these letters are a top priority and the relationship managers are always very good at getting back to me. Sticking to the approved language of the template speeds up the approval/signature process in the principal's office since they know what to expect."

Logan tracks the letters on a spreadsheet that is a revised version of the monthly report of gifts. She adds the Comments column, inserts the name of the relationship manager, and yes or no if the donor wants a letter of thanks. She adds the date the draft was sent for approval and name of the person the letter was given to in the principal's office.

"It is really quite a collaborative process and I think that is what makes it successful," Logan says. "We are all responsible for ensuring the donor receives a letter that will make them feel good about their gift."

Source: Karen Logan, Stewardship Officer, Queen's University, Summerhill, Kingston, Ontario, Canada. Phone (613) 533-2060, ext. 74122. E-mail: karen.logan@queensu.ca

The stewardship officer at Queen's University (Summerhill, Kingston, Ontario) uses this Microsoft Excel spreadsheet to track gifts of $100,000 or more and acknowledgment letters sent to the donors.

Content not available in this edition

Gift Acknowledgment Protocols Reduce Confusion, Lessen Mistakes

Scott Fendley, Principal, SF Consulting (Eden Prairie, MN), shares a detailed acknowledgment policy he developed for Wabash College (Crawfordsville, IN):

PROTOCOL FOR CAMPAIGN GIFT Acknowledgment

The baseline or default response to gifts and/or pledges is:

All gifts to the College will be acknowledged by an official receipt thank you letter within two working days of the arrival of the gift on campus.

Annual donors of $250-999 will receive a letter from the Chair of the ...Foundation at the beginning of the month after the gift is received. ...

Donors of $1,000+ will receive a letter from the Chair of the 1832 Society at the beginning of the month after the gift is received. (Trustees will not receive this letter). Any changes in gift club status will be noted.

Phonathon pledges will be acknowledged in writing immediately after the pledge is made via handwritten note from student caller who took the pledge.

The Director of the Greater Wabash Foundation will acknowledge all pledges (excluding phonathon pledges) of $1-999. ... within 48 hours of receipt.

The Dean for Advancement will review all gifts and pledge payments of $1,000 and above and add personal acknowledgments, as appropriate, within 48 hours of receipt of the gift or pledge payment.

The Chairman of the Campaign will acknowledge outright gifts and pledges of $10,000 and above.

Documented bequests, trusts, life insurance gifts, and other planned giving vehicles that have been confirmed (not matured) shall be acknowledged by the Director of Major Gifts within 48 hours of notification for all gifts up to $100,000. The Dean for Advancement shall acknowledge any confirmed planned gift of $100,000 and above. The Dean for Advancement and the Director of Major and Planned Giving will advise the President of the College regarding the donors he should acknowledge.

The President of the College will be provided a list of all donors who have made a gift of $1,000 or more for his personal acknowledgments.

The Dean for Advancement will acknowledge all gifts and pledges from trustees and members of the board of the National Association of Wabash Men....

The Dean for Advancement and Chairman of the Faculty/Staff Campaign will acknowledge any pledge or gift made by a faculty or staff member. ...

The Dean for Advancement will acknowledge any gift from the Independent Colleges of Indiana.

The Senior Advancement Officer and Coordinator of Volunteer Services will acknowledge any gifts from non-alumni or non-parent owned corporations and all foundations, excluding matching gifts from corporations.

When a matching gift is received, a letter to the donor will be generated and signed by the Director of the Greater Wabash Foundation, excluding trustees. Matching gift companies will receive a receipt only.

Any alumni-owned or parent-owned business that makes a gift will be acknowledged as if the individual owner made the gift.

Letters acknowledging the receipt of memorial gifts, without specifying the gift amount, will be sent to the appropriate person in the family by the Dean for Advancement once a month.

When a gift of stock is made, the valuation ...will be included in the receipt thank you letter, which will be signed by the Dean for Advancement.

If volunteers give their expenses to the College as an in-kind gift instead of reimbursement, the Senior Advancement Officer and Coordinator of Volunteer Services will acknowledge the gift with a thank you letter.

Upon receipt of the final pledge payment (excluding phonathon pledges), a letter of acknowledgment from the Dean for Advancement will be generated thanking the donor for the completion of the pledge.

All letters will be changed quarterly, or as needed to refresh the content and reflect on recent news of the College. These letters will be prepared or reviewed by the Director of Campaign Communications.

(The policy also includes sections detailing special recognition of gifts, as well as how to issue pledge reminders.)

Acknowledging major gifts on the fly may cause important details to fall through the cracks, says Scott Fendley, principal, SF Consulting (Eden Prairie, MN).

That's why organizations should put gift acknowledgment policies in writing. Says Fendley, "Written acknowledgment policies prevent confusion, duplication of efforts, and 'I thought someone else did that,' kinds of situations."

Create policies that are as detailed as possible, he says. Specifically, gift acknowledgment forms should:

- Codify individual staff roles for as many common situations as possible.
- Describe in detail (mailings, signatures, time frames) responses to all gift sizes and program(s) supported.
- Clarify what donors will be invited to what events at what level for different gifts.

Granularity is also important in effective policies, Fendley says, enabling database software to be programmed to automate response actions while ensuring a continuity of response as development staff come and go.

Acknowledgment protocols are particularly useful with more esoteric planned giving vehicles such as memorial gifts, says Fendley, noting that heirs and survivors can be easily overlooked or forgotten.

Acknowledgment policies are best developed by advancement staff with input from senior leadership, says Fendley, and should include input from services and operations staff, as these departments are often involved with implementing, automating, and executing policies.

Source: Scott Fendley, Principal, SF Consulting, Eden Prairie, MN. Phone (317) 445-0948. E-mail: scott@sfconsultingnow.com. Website: www.sfconsultingnow.com

Common Mistakes in Acknowledging Gifts

A few mistakes in acknowledging gifts are common to many nonprofits, says Scott Fendley, principal of SF Consulting (Eden Prairie, MN). Among these are:

✓ **Too personalized.** "Personalization is good, but taking two weeks to acknowledge a $50 gift because the cards all have to be hand-signed is not a sustainable system."

✓ **Written letters for online gifts.** "For online gifts below $1,000, there is no reason you couldn't automate electronic acknowledgments which would include all the proper IRS language."

✓ **Not acknowledging the total gift.** "With things like annuities and charitable remainders, organizations can become so involved in following the details of tax law that they end up acknowledging IRS-figured numbers instead of the total amount the donor actually gave."

Which Form of Thanks Would You Prefer?

If you were to make a gift to a charity, which form of gift acknowledgment would you prefer receiving:

A. A form letter "personalized" by a computer and mailed within 24 hours of the charity receiving your gift, or

B. A handwritten note of appreciation from a key staff member, client or volunteer, sent within a week of receipt of your gift?

The answer "B" would probably be your first choice, but many development shops don't operate that way.

Look at how you acknowledge gifts. Are your gestures as personal as possible? Or could you improve your efforts to make people feel the true impact their gifts make?

How Do You Say 'Thanks'?

When a donor makes a gift, especially a major gift, it's not enough to say, "We really appreciate your support." Donors hear that phrase all the time.

Go beyond the expected. Put yourself in the shoes of the donor and offer a more personal gesture of gratitude: "I told our board chair about your recent gift and she called you 'an angel.'"

E-mail Blast Thanks Donors, Links Them to News on What Their Gifts Make Possible

Use the latest technology to thank donors and underscore how their gifts boost your mission.

Stewardship staff at The Hill School (Pottstown, PA), sent an e-mail blast to all donors in December 2008 as an additional thank-you for their gifts over the past year. The e-mail linked to the school's website, which had the same message enhanced with a slideshow of students on campus.

"The e-mail message thanked all donors, annual and capital, and informed them about projects that their contributions had helped support," says Erin Genn, assistant director of stewardship. "Publicly recognizing our current donors on our website was also beneficial because it acted as a reminder and further encouragement for other constituents who had not yet made a gift."

Stewardship staff sent the e-mail to all donors for whom the school had e-mail addresses and posted the content of the e-mail on the school's homepage for donors for whom they did not have e-mail addresses but who visit the website, she says.

Genn shares advice for implementing this stewardship strategy:

❑ Make sure you have a way to also reach donors who have not shared e-mail addresses with you.

❑ Use an e-mail account designated for e-mail blasts, not your personal or main work e-mail address.

❑ Keep it short and to the point. "We edited the message in the e-mail, but

included a link to our website which provided more details and the photo slideshow," she says.

Source: Erin Genn, Assistant Director of Stewardship, The Hill School, Pottstown, PA. Phone (610) 705-1059. E-mail: egenn@thehill.org

This e-mail blast provided a year-end thank-you to donors to The Hill School (Pottstown, PA) as well as let them know how their gifts help support the school.

Content not available in this edition

Analyze Your Pledge Acknowledgment Process

Whether you're in the midst of a capital campaign or in an ongoing process of seeking major gifts, do you have a system that all staff follow for acknowledging major gift pledges as they are made?

Some charity officials may think they have a process in place, but upon closer examination, find glitches in the system, or that not everyone is adhering to the process.

Answers to these questions will help point out whether your acknowledgment process needs fine-tuning:

- Is a formal pledge signed the moment a verbal commitment is made?

- Who receives copies of the signed pledge?

- Is a letter of thanks sent out to the donor within 48 hours?

- Who sends a letter of thanks or makes a personal phone call to the donor? Is there a chain of command involved with various levels of gifts?

- When a pledge is received, what entries are made in the donor's database file? By whom?

- Does staff training include a review of the pledge acknowledgment process?

Good Stewardship Matters

Who says timeliness and the personal touch don't count?

One retired physician decided he would begin contributing $1,000 annually to his community's two hospitals.

Officials at one hospital foundation were quick to get a personal note of appreciation out the door within 24 hours after receipt of the gift. The other hospital sent a preprinted thank-you postcard several days later.

This pattern of gift acknowledgment was repeated each year the physician gave his gift.

The retired doctor decided to make a $500,000 gift. Guess where it went? That's right. The entire gift went to the hospital that had always followed up with a personal message promptly, and with a personal touch.

Make a Personal Phone Call to All First-time Donors

Making new donors feel appreciated can lead them to be longtime donors.

Erica Hart, assistant director of scholarships and annual giving at Georgia Perimeter College (Decatur, GA), says she calls all new donors (except corporate and foundation donors) within three days of the receipt of their gift. She doesn't use a script, but simply introduces herself and says, "I wanted to thank you for your recent gift in support of (area the gift supports)." She tells them about the program and asks them to update their information. If no one answers she leaves the information in a voice mail.

"I check the year they graduated, their major, what teachers they were involved with, and ask them about their memories of the college," she says. "They are more than willing to talk because it's not a solicitation call. Most

donors are surprised by the call. Some say, 'It was only a small gift,' or 'I know it's not much.' Many say 'Thank you for calling me.' Sometimes they have questions. If I can't answer them, I will pass the question on to someone who can and then follow up to make sure it was answered."

The information she collects is passed on to the alumni department. It is also tracked in an action tab in Raiser's Edge, fundraising software by Blackbaud, Inc.

Persons who give more than $1,000 are also contacted by the director of institutional advancement by phone or letter, says Hart.

Source: Erica Hart, Assistant Director of Scholarships and Annual Giving at Georgia Perimeter College, Decatur, GA. Phone (678) 891-2559. E-mail: Erica.Hart@gpc.edu

GIFT ACKNOWLEDGMENT PROCEDURES

How Do You Acknowledge Anonymous Gifts?

John Carroll University (University Heights, OH) recently received a $4.45 million anonymous bequest — the largest anonymous gift by an individual in the university's 124-year history — to support scholarships.

"We spent some time with the donor to understand why she didn't want to be named and then determined what we could do to recognize the gift commitment that would respect her wishes," says Doreen Knapp Riley, vice president for advancement.

They chose to use a press release to announce the anonymous gift, along with a small thank-you dinner with the donor's family, university president and board chair. The donor saw and approved the press release before it was sent out and was also told where and when it would be sent, says Riley.

"The donor understands the value of philanthropy and how announcing the gift and its purpose, in the form of a press release, might encourage others to give scholarship gifts," she says.

The donor was also involved in selecting the date, time and place of the thank-you dinner, as well as who would be invited, says Riley. "We sat down with her and discussed, 'This is what we are planning, what do you think?' to make sure that she was comfortable with everything."

At the dinner the person most respected by the donor will acknowledge the gift and the donor's commitment to the institution, she says.

The donor's anonymity is respected at every step, says Riley. For instance:

✓ Very few people know the identity of the donor.

✓ Very little information is included in the donor's record.

✓ A code is used in place of the donor's name in the gift file and only two people know where the file is located.

✓ The president and board chair acknowledge the gift.

"Every donor is unique and wants to be acknowledged in a different way," says Riley. "When it comes to donor recognition and stewardship, we want to do whatever the donor is comfortable with and is appropriate for the university."

Source: Doreen Knapp Riley, Vice President for University Advancement, John Carroll University, University Heights, OH. Phone (216) 397-4345. E-mail: driley@jcu.edu

Stewardship Essentials: The Donor Relations Guide.
Edited by Scott C. Stevenson.
© 2011 Stevenson, Inc. Published 2011 by Stevenson, Inc.

Stewardship Essentials: The Donor Relations Guide

DONOR RECOGNITION AS AN ACT OF STEWARDSHIP

In addition to immediate gift acknowledgment, donor recognition is also a first step in the stewardship process. Prompt recognition should accompany any gift, major or otherwise. The type of recognition you choose will be driven by the level of support but should fairly and openly recognize donors for their generosity (unless they choose to remain anonymous).

Recognizing Your Top Donor

Q. *"What do you do to recognize your most significant donor in a significant way?"*

"At the American Diabetes Association and with our Research Foundation, we have a standard set of recognition opportunities (personal tours during our scientific sessions, names in annual reports and ads in our consumer publication, Diabetes Forecast). But what makes our stewardship unique is that our stewardship director will discuss with our staff member and our donor ways that are meaningful to him or her. For example, we don't own a building, but we do have research grants that can be named in honor of the donor. Then each time the researcher is published, we give the donor copies of the article. We will also arrange personal lab tours at private gatherings for the donor and the scientists."

— Elly Brtva, Managing Director of Individual Gifts,
American Diabetes Association (Alexandria, VA)

"This past year, the office of medical development raised several endowed professorships (each professorship is a $4 million gift). At a small dinner of about 50 people hosted by the dean of the medical school, we recognize the donor and the faculty who will be the chair holder. The donor and faculty member each receives a professorship medal and Stanford chair in addition to a professionally designed photo album commemorating the evening."

— Lorraine Alexander, Senior Director of Development,
Neuroscience Institute, Stanford University (Menlo Park, CA)

"The Minneapolis Institute of Arts has a long-time trustee and major benefactor who has made countless gifts over his lifetime. During the opening of our new wing, we honored him and his legacy of support by announcing a permanent art endowment in his name. His fellow trustees had contributed nearly $4 million to this art endowment as a tribute to his decades of generosity.

"As a result, the museum — and the community — now have a permanent testament to this donor's commitment to excellence in our collections."

—Joan Grathwol Olson, Director of Development, The
Minneapolis Institute of Arts (Minneapolis, MN)

Honor Top Supporters With a Recognition Award

Missouri State University already offered several awards for academic giving, employee support and the like. Why did university officials need another?

To recognize a very important constituency, Brent Dunn, vice president of university advancement, says in explaining MSU's Bronze Bear Award.

"The award recognizes people who have had a major and ongoing impact on the university, whether through service, financial support or both," Dunn says. "It honors a lifetime of service."

Recipients are endorsed by the university administrative council, faculty senate, staff senate and student government association before being approved by the board of governors. Recipients are presented with a framed resolution and 18-inch, 45-pound bronze bear statuette at winter commencement proceedings and invited to address the graduating class.

Working to maximize recognition for both the recipients and the university, officials publicize both the Board of Governors' approval in October and the December presentation ceremony.

Dunn says the award not only honors past supporters, it inspires new ones.

"Bronze Bear recipients include past university presidents, former members of the Board of Governors and nationally recognized philanthropists. It's a very prestigious group," he says. "Winning an award is not what moves people to serve, but it does establish a great level of support that others might strive to emulate."

Source: Brent Dunn, Vice President for University Advancement,
Missouri State University, Springfield, MO. Phone (417) 836-6666.
E-mail: brentdunn@missouristate.edu

DONOR RECOGNITION AS AN ACT OF STEWARDSHIP

Limiting Award Recipients Adds Value to Honor

Q. How do you recognize your most generous donors?

"(We do so) with our Texas Star Awards. The award has been in place for more than five years and honors those individuals or corporations who have demonstrated outstanding generosity and community involvement. The most recent one was given to a family foundation that made a leadership gift to The Hawks Family Foundation Wishing Place, contributed as one of the premier supporters of our Wish Night auction and had two members serve terms on our governing board.

"We don't give the award just to give it. It is not given every year — only when there are appropriate candidates. There have only been three recipients in the chapter's history.

"(When giving donor awards), it is important to have clear guidelines of who is eligible for any award program, which helps to ensure that the review process is selective and that the award retains its value."

— Erin Michel, Development Director-Central Region, Make-A-Wish Foundation of North Texas (Irving, TX)

Feature Donor/Gift Profiles

Regularly include donor gift profiles in each issue of your constituency newsletter or magazine as well as on your website. Doing so is a great way to publicly recognize the generosity of major donors and also serves to plant the seeds of philanthropy in others' minds on an ongoing basis.

Although it's important to focus on the donor and what motivated him/her to contribute, it's even more important to give ink to the impact that the gift is having or will have on your organization and those it serves.

Another benefit of donor profiles is they help to improve readership of your publications and website. People enjoy reading about others' gifts — how they came about, why the donor decided to fund a particular project and how that gift is making a difference.

Use these communications venues to shine a spotlight on various ways donors have made gifts to illustrate the possibilities available: gifts of property, gifts of stock, annuities and more.

Seek Donor Direction When Publicizing Momentous Gifts

When promoting a major gift, structure gift announcements according to donor specifications, says Wendy Walker Zeller, director of donor relations and communications for Washburn Endowment Association, the fundraising arm of Washburn University (Topeka, KS).

By properly publicizing major gifts with your donor's wishes in mind, you are letting the donor know how important his/her gift is while increasing the possibility of the donor making another gift to your organization at a later date, says Zeller.

"What the donor wants is foremost in our minds," Zeller says. "If they are unsure, we offer suggestions based on the intention of the gift — where they are making the gift, etc."

Make the gift announcement event pleasing and rewarding for the donor by meeting his/her needs and expectations, says Zeller. Washburn staff work directly with donors to create the experience the donors would like to have at the gift announcement, she says. If a donor will not be present for the announcement, she says, they ask for the donor's input and then share the details of the plan with the donor.

"We try to make the experience a good one for the media as well, keeping in mind the best time of day and most comfortable location to hold a press conference," she says, "ensuring we have adequate lighting and sound and giving access to the donor for questions (if donor is present and willing)."

When possible, says Zeller, they also prepare a press packet for the media that contains background information for the story.

News releases announcing major gifts are sent to a broad media list, including media outlets that reflect the donor's personal history such as the donor's hometown and the town where his/her employer is headquartered.

Source: Wendy Walker Zeller, Director of Donor Relations & Communications, Washburn Endowment Association, Topeka, KS. Phone (785) 670-4483. E-mail: wwalker@wea.org

DONOR RECOGNITION AS AN ACT OF STEWARDSHIP

Create Policy for Publicizing Momentous Gifts as First Step in Stewarding Donors

Take inspiration from these two organizations to publicize your next major gift:

Share Announcement With Those Who Will Benefit From It Most

Washburn University (Topeka, KS) recently received its largest single gift from an individual — a $5 million gift from Trish and Richard Davidson to supplement faculty salaries in its School of Business.

To publicize the momentous gift, Washburn officials turned to the university policy that calls for all gift announcements to be structured to the donor's specifications, says Wendy Walker Zeller, director of donor relations and communications for the Washburn Endowment Association, Washburn University's fundraising arm.

The Davidsons wanted to be present for this gift announcement, Zeller says, "so we spent a great deal of time working out the details to meet their wishes." The Davidsons asked to speak to a class of business students. Also attending the class? The news media, along with the university president, endowment association president, business school dean and board of regents chair. The 100-some students were invited to stay for the gift announcement, which took place just after the press arrived in the classroom.

Media received press packets featuring the Davidsons' biography and were seated at the front of the classroom. A backdrop with the university logo and drape displaying the business school were arranged for the announcement.

"The students gave a spontaneous standing ovation following the announcement, which was filmed by a couple of the local TV stations," she says.

Following the gift announcement, says Zeller, the media were invited to interview the donors in a separate location against a backdrop of the university logo.

"Other than a few people on campus and several trustees, we kept the gift amount and identity of the donors under wraps until the official announcement, which helped build suspense and pique press interest," she says. She plans to include an article about the gift in the endowment's annual report and the next issue of the alumni magazine.

Carefully Time Release of News to Maximize Publicity, Impact

Chatham Hall (Chatham, VA), an independent college prepa-

ratory high school for girls, recently received a $31 million gift from the estate of Elizabeth Beckwith Nilsen, a former student. The gift was the largest single gift to any girls' independent school.

Because of the magnitude of the gift, Melissa Evans Fountain, director of the office of advancement, says they followed this special plan of action in publicizing it:

On announcement day, classes were delayed until 9:30 a.m. From 8 to 9 a.m., the president of the board and head of school announced the gift to the faculty and answered questions about the gift. At 9 a.m., faculty were joined by the staff and students, and the head of school and board president announced the gift to this larger group.

Staff sent a news release at 9:15 a.m. through US 1 Premium Newswire, the Philanthropy Microlist and the Education Microlist and posted it on the school's website.

At 9:30 a.m., after the all-school meeting, the head of Chatham Hall sent an e-mail announcing the gift to all major educational associations, suggesting they share the news with their constituents.

From 9:30 to 10:30 a.m., calls were made to members of the Alumnae Council and Parent Advisory Council, past heads of the school, certain major donors and other VIPs (all trustees and several top donors knew about the gift prior to the announcement).

At 10:30 a.m. an e-mail blast was sent to all constituents in the school's database and the announcement was posted on the school's Facebook page.

That same day, college officials mailed a press release to donor prospects (alumnae, parents and friends) with a cover letter announcing the gift in the context of the school's capital campaign. They also sent the press release to state and local VIPs, area leaders in the Episcopal Church (with which the college is affiliated) and an admission office list that included prospective students and educational consultants. A special article was also written for the school's fall 2009 alumnae magazine.

Sources: Melissa Evans Fountain, Director of the Office of Advancement, Chatham Hall, Chatham, VA. Phone (434) 432-5549. E-mail: mfountain@chathamhall.org
Wendy Walker Zeller, Director of Donor Relations & Communications, Washburn Endowment Association, Topeka, KS. Phone (785) 670-4483. E-mail: wwalker@wea.org

DONOR RECOGNITION AS AN ACT OF STEWARDSHIP

Don't Underestimate the Power of a Donor Wall

You might not think a prominently displayed donor wall that lists major donors' names would provide much incentive for others to give. But it does.

Be sure all marketing efforts state that anyone who gives above a certain level will have his/her name(s) listed on a handsome donor wall to be permanently displayed in a prominent location.

Consider going a step further to say that names will be categorized into three levels of giving.

Although a permanent display in and of itself may not motivate a major gift, it can influence someone's decision to give generously, and it serves as a great way to recognize donors who make principal gifts.

Recognition Gallery of Honor Showcases Donors

Consider creating a recognition wall to permanently honor your major donors.

Since 2004, persons who give $5,000 or more to Carroll Hospital Center (Westminster, MD) have had their names placed on its Gallery of Honor, a 20-foot wide, five-foot tall recognition wall located in the most visible spot in the hospital — the outer lobby.

Sherri Hosfeld Joseph, director of development, says they created the display to encourage donors' giving and inspire them to give more and reach to achieve a higher level on the display. Cumulative giving amounts are based on gifts made since 1989, which she says is as far back as the foundation's electronic records go.

"We make sure our consistent donors are aware of the wall, and let new donors know that a gift at a certain level will get them on the wall," she says. "We also place brochures in a rack by the wall so that visitors can grab one if they are interested in knowing how to make a gift."

The honor wall recognizes eight giving levels:

1. Chairman's Circle, $1 million or more
2. Sinnott Fellows, $500,000 to $999,999
3. President's Club, $250,000 to $499,999
4. 1961 Society, $100,000 to $249,999
5. Stewards Club, $50,000 to $99,999
6. Galen Club, $25,000 to $49,999
7. Sponsor, $10,000 to $24,999
8. Patron, $5,000 to $9,999

When donors make gifts that move them up a giving level, Hosfeld Joseph says, development staff place new name plaques in the appropriate giving spots, then send the old plaques to the donors as a gift, along with an invitation to come see the gallery.

Donors who include the hospital in estate plans are honored on the wall under a Bridge Builders listing.

Development staff add names to the wall twice a year by running a cumulative giving report of $5,000-plus, says Hosfeld Joseph. The magnetic plaques, engraved with donors' names, cost $25 to $80, depending on the size.

Source: Sherri Hosfeld Joseph, Director of Development, Carroll Hospital Center & Carroll Hospice, Westminster, MD. Phone (410) 871-6200. E-mail: Sjoseph@carrollhospitalcenter.org

Prominently featured in the outer lobby of Carroll Hospital Center (Westminster, MD), this donor wall recognizes persons who make cumulative gifts of $5,000 and more.

Content not available in this edition

DONOR RECOGNITION AS AN ACT OF STEWARDSHIP

Make 'Philanthropist of the Year' Award a Special Occasion

Being recognized as Philanthropist of the Year — as many local chapters of the Association of Fundraising Professionals (AFP), Arlington, VA, as well as numerous individual nonprofits, do for major donors — is of course a special event for the recipient.

How can you help make the presentation of such an honor even more special?

Here are some real-life suggestions from local AFP chapters nationwide:

"Our chapter has always provided the honoree with a specially made scrapbook with more than 100 letters, notes and photographs inside. Once an honoree is chosen, we get in touch with his or her family, friends, and all the nonprofits he or she is involved with, to ask for letters of congratulations, of memories, etc. The scrapbook often has old photos, newspaper articles, and letters from the mayor and governor. It always includes the invitation and the program from the honoring ceremony. Many times, it has drawings from the honoree's children and grandchildren. Honorees have told us that they keep it out at all times. It becomes a treasured family keepsake."

— *Del Martin, Philanthropist of the Year Award Chairperson, Greater Atlanta Chapter (Atlanta, GA)*

"Every other year, our local chapter hosts a big awards ceremony and luncheon on National Philanthropy Day to recognize Outstanding Philanthropist, Outstanding Volunteer Fundraiser, Outside Youth/Youth Group in Philanthropy, Outside AFP Chapter Member Philanthropist and Outstanding Planned Giving Philanthropist. On the off years, we hold a smaller, more intimate luncheon where we invite the Outstanding Philanthropist recipient from the previous year to come as the guest speaker and share his or her story. Spreading the recognition over two years makes it more meaningful, as the Outstanding Philanthropist has usually been involved in community philanthropy for many years."

— *Jenni Venema, Director of Development, Illinois Quad Cities Chapter (Moline, IL)*

"Each of our five philanthropy awards is presented to the current honoree by a past honoree. In addition, the past honoree who serves as presenter is asked to elaborate on the current honoree's philanthropy. This has proven meaningful to our honorees — they get to hear how their work inspires others, and feel a part of the philanthropic community."

— *Martha E. Connor, Vice President of Programming, Yosemite Valley Chapter (Modesto, CA)*

Tips for Published Donor Lists

To help build a habit of annual giving and increased loyalty, include the consecutive number of years a donor has contributed when you publish your annual honor roll of contributors. Here is an example:

8	Mark Brown
1	Mr. and Mrs. Herman Goodenow
15	Susan Haegger
1	Kurt Trucking
5	Rick & Company
2	Mary and Mick Urbansky

Donors take pride in seeing that number grow next to their names.

Stewardship Essentials: The Donor Relations Guide

PERSONALIZING ACTS OF STEWARDSHIP

Anyone who has made a significant gift to your charity deserves both personal and genuine attention. Consider The Golden Rule as you steward donors. How would you like to be treated if you chose to share your good fortune with others? If, for example, you were in a position to make a $100,000 gift, how would you wish to be treated?

Tailor Appreciation Gifts to Donors' Unique Interests

All too often, charities produce a framed photograph or certificate or purchase some other memento in mass quantities to thank donors for generous support, only to have the item end up in the donor's closet or round file.

Rather than take that approach to recognize your important donors, develop a depository of unique but not overly expensive items from which to draw for special donors.

Use this two-pronged approach to match appreciation/cultivation gifts to both prospects and donors:

1. Learn and make note of prospects' unique likes and interests early in the cultivation process. One prospect may talk about a longtime interest in matchbooks while another may mention a fondness for her English heritage. Those clues will alert you to be on the lookout for items that may not cost much but may mean a great deal to the prospect.

2. Either develop a list of unique gift items or purchase items from time to time that can be part of a depository from which to select special gifts for special persons.

Unique Gifts for Donors, Prospects

Here's a small sampling of gift ideas for major gift donors to help you develop an appropriate list of your own:

1. **Items native to your region.** For native sons and daughters who no longer live in your community, consider items unique to your city, state or region (e.g., maple syrup, regional books, a subscription to a regional magazine, print from a local artist).

2. **Collectors' items:** Old postcards, thimbles, glassware, sports memorabilia, canes, more.

3. **Gifts for donors' loved ones (including pets).** Sometimes donors are even more touched by a gift directed to someone important in their lives other than themselves: grandchildren, a spouse or even a beloved pet.

4. **Difficult-to-come-by items.** Just being aware of donors' interests will help you spot a unique or hard-to-come-by item during your travels and everyday experiences — a ticket to a particular event, a gift certificate to a bed and breakfast and other such items.

Try This Stewardship Idea

Do you have a list of dates identifying when significant gifts were made to your organization?

Go through past records to determine significant major gift dates. Then, on the anniversary of each gift, plan to send an anniversary letter to the donor (or children of the donor), reminding them of what a difference that gift has made in the life of your institution.

Your appreciation won't go unnoticed.

Recognize the Power Of a Personal Note

With cell phones, e-mail and other forms of communication bombarding our daily lives, the old-fashioned personal note — sent via postal service — is taking on more meaning.

You can't beat a handwritten note to convey sincerity. It takes time to write and mail a personal message, and that's exactly why it means more than other forms of communication. Set a daily or weekly goal for sending handwritten notes to constituents. Without question, they will get noticed.

Focus on Donors Individually When Recognizing Major Gifts

Q. We are holding an event at which we will be recognizing two donors, one who gave $1 million, and one who gave $100,000. How do we recognize both donors appropriately at the same event?

"Hold separate recognition ceremonies that feature each donor. You wouldn't want to have the ceremonies at the same time because it would mean both donors would be sharing the spotlight, which wouldn't be in the best interest of the donor who gave the larger amount. If you have to hold the ceremonies at the same time, you might want to host a private luncheon or dinner with the president and the $1 million donor and his or her family either before or following the event. This elevates the larger donor's generosity to a higher level. The lower-level donor could be invited to a luncheon or dinner with the dean of the school benefiting from the gift."

— *Leanne Poon, Manager, Donor Relations & Stewardship, University of British Columbia (Vancouver, British Columbia, Canada)*

"Dollar level alone cannot decide the course of action. At either of those donation levels, you should have some idea of the relationship of gift size to potential as well as what's most meaningful to and in keeping with the personality of the donor.

"The $100,000 gift might have been an extreme stretch for that donor, the most they can ever give. The $1 million gift might have been a moderate or even 'typical' gift for the other donor. Each donor knows which category he or she is in. If the smaller gift was a stretch gift and the larger donor gets more recognition, what message does that convey about the values of your organization?

"There are more folks out there who might be able to consider a $100,000 gift — even as a stretch gift — under certain circumstances than a $1 million gift. Don't make the prize too out of reach for them."

— *Mary Kay Filter Dietrich, Vice President for Development & External Relations, Urban League of Greater Pittsburgh (Pittsburgh, PA)*

Engage Donor's Family in Recognition Efforts

When an individual or couple makes a major gift, ask for permission to involve their adult children in recognizing the gift. Doing so will serve as an important first step in cultivating those heirs to one day make similar gifts or to add to an existing family gift.

You can involve a donor's family by:

1. Inviting input on ways their parents might be recognized. Share some recognition options on which they can comment.

2. Making sure the entire family gets VIP treatment during any recognition events or ceremonies that take place: seating, public introductions and more.

3. Including the children in ongoing stewardship efforts: periodic reports on the impact of their parent's gift, invitations to your organization's events and so forth.

Get Creative When Sharing Gift's Impact With Donor

Q. What is a creative way to share the impact of a major gift with the donor who made it all happen?

"When the gift is intangible but still life-changing, like a scholarship, I've helped a couple charities to share the very personal impact on a life. With the parties' permissions, a professional researcher/writer is commissioned to write the life story of the donor and the recipient. The resulting work is published in short form and provided to each in detail as

'life lived, life changed, lives connected forever.' Not only does this have a deep impact on the donor, but the recipient is often inspired to one day become a philanthropist himself. The first time I tried this in a very small way, the recipient — a student — ended up establishing his own fund and is donating to it as a recent graduate!"

— *Paul Nazareth, Manager, Planned and Personal Giving, Catholic Archdiocese of Toronto, (Toronto, Ontario, Canada)*

Four Ways to Express Heartfelt Appreciation on a Budget

When it's time to pay special tribute to someone highly important to your organization, remember that some of the most meaningful gifts of appreciation are those that require creativity, time and input from a variety of people, but not necessarily a lot of cash.

Chances are the person you are honoring already has a wall filled with plaques, inscribed crystal paperweights and engraved silver bowls. Rather than looking to add to this collection, seek instead a way to create a more meaningful form of recognition.

Here are ideas to get you started on your personalized recognition:

Make a This-is-your-life Video

Create and produce an amateur video of your honoree's life featuring highlights of involvement in your organization. Interview friends, volunteers, administrators, board members and others whose lives have been touched in a positive way. Show results of projects the honoree has helped complete and the impact those projects have had on persons your organization serves. Include video of photos of the honoree in a candid moment, or working with others — but let the honoree believe it's for another purpose until you are ready to screen your production.

Create a Commemorative Work of Art

If you have a skilled artist among your volunteer base, ask the person to draw a portrait of the honoree as part of a collage spotlighting his or her accomplishments for your organization. Invest in quality framing so the recipient will be proud to display it.

Or you may wish to create a simpler but equally heartfelt project. Gather young artists (children you serve, or children of your staff or volunteers) to paint a large mural to present to your honored supporter. You also can ask them to paint individual works following a theme, then assemble and present the works in a large bound book.

Another idea: Engage talented adult volunteers to create a group project, such as a set of holiday ornaments, hand-painted glassware or beautiful needlepoint. If they sew, each could create a square for a colorful quilt.

Make a Memory Book

Buy a large, well-made scrapbook (with room for additional pages) and fill with photos, mementos such as event programs, ribbons, badges, news clippings and special items to provide a timeline of your honoree's involvement. Ask friends and family to help locate photos.

Chances are several of your volunteers are quite skilled at scrapbooking and would be happy to create a multi-paged work of art for your honoree using the many themed stickers, picture anchors and creative papers available.

Ask everyone in your organization who knows the honoree to sign the book, and even write messages of congratulations and appreciation, high school yearbook-style.

Give Special Donors Their Own Special Day

Make a proclamation to hold an annual Pat Johnson Day at your institution on a date that is important to your honoree. Have your chief executive officer, board members and other appropriate officials and even your mayor sign the certificate. To add even more meaning, mark that special day as an annual date for your institution to do something meaningful in the recipient's honor, like begin an annual campaign, host a luncheon or start a canned food drive.

Make the Best Use of Donor Photos

When donors visit your premises to attend a banquet, meet the recipient of their gifts or view a project they recently helped to fund, picture-taking is generally included among the activities that take place. But what happens with those donor photos once they have been developed? Do they end up on a shelf, never to be seen again?

Here are some options for making the best use of donor photos:

✓ Send a photo of the donor to the donor along with a personal note of gratitude.
✓ If the donor's gift helped a particular person — scholarship recipient, patient, youth — send the recipient a photo of the donor with a note saying, "Perhaps you will be able to assist someone one day, just as this person assisted you."
✓ Keep a photo in the donor's file so staff can familiarize themselves with who's who, should the donor make a visit or a new development officer is scheduled to meet the donor somewhere for the first time.
✓ Develop a feature story or profile to accompany each photo that can be pitched to the media. Maintain an up-to-date file of feature possibilities.
✓ Maintain a yearly photo album in your lobby or a bulletin board that depicts your organization's ties to its many donors.

Thank Donors With Exclusive Experience

Donor gifts can be challenging. Some donors love them, others hate them, and some just think they're a waste of the money they are contributing.

So how do you show your donors the love without alienating them? Try offering them a one-of-a-kind experience. Take the guesswork out of giving by trying some of the ideas listed below:

✓ Are you opening a new building, unveiling a new exhibit or getting a new piece of equipment? Invite your donors to see it first.

✓ Is someone famous coming to speak at one of your events? Have you hired a celebrity to make an appearance to benefit your organization? Try to set up a small group experience between your donors and the celebrity.

✓ Does your organization deliver meals to the elderly or run play groups for disadvantaged children? Ask your donors if they would like to help.

✓ Do you have a black-tie fundraiser coming up? Offer your donors discounted tickets, exclusive seating or a preview of auction items.

✓ Having a gold party, jewelry sale or garage sale? Invite your donors to preview the goods before anyone else.

✓ Is your organization home to some cool or interesting jobs? Donors can be doctors for a day or join your head coach on the bench or in the locker room for a behind-the-scenes look at a major sporting event.

Stewardship Essentials: The Donor Relations Guide

STEWARDSHIP PROTOCOL AND ETHICS

Stewardship is embodied in a sacred trust between the donor and your organization and those representing your organization. That trust must include the highest of ethical standards embracing values such as fidelity to the principles of stewardship, accountability and transparency to donors, honesty, integrity, respect and more.

Being Forthright Will Always Win Out

For most development officers, the pressure to produce is always present: Make the ask, meet your monthly quota and go for as much as possible. In spite of that ongoing pressure, don't forget what matters most: maintaining the highest degree of ethics, always being honest and taking a long-term approach when dealing with prospects and donors.

While forces outside of your control may be encouraging you to go for broke in cultivating gifts, think long-term: "I want this donor to feel so good about her gift commitment that she'll be inclined to give even more at a later date."

As you meet with and cultivate relationships with would-be donors, be mindful of their circumstances. Your timing for a gift may not be the best timing for them. Your need for a gift directed toward a particular project may not be what turns them on most. The more sensitive you can be to their world, the more successful you will ultimately be in your work. Plus, your career will be a much more fulfilling experience.

Clarify Ethics Expectations With Your Staff

A handful of nonprofit organizations that may lack fundraising integrity throughout the nation make it difficult for those nonprofits that strive every day to operate in an ethical way.

That's all the more reason for you to continually stress fundraising ethics among your organization's staff.

Empower members of your development team to be examples of the highest ethical standards by:

1. Reviewing national standards of fundraising ethics. (See examples published by the Association of Fundraising Professionals: www.afpnet.org/ethics)

2. Sharing selected readings that review fundraising ethics. (See The Foundation Center's examples: http://fdncenter.org/learn/topical/ethics.html)

3. Creating and documenting a set of ethics tailored specifically to your nonprofit organization.

Equally important, regularly recognize those employees who are examples of the highest integrity and don't hesitate to act swiftly when persons violate ethical standards of your organization.

Adhere to the Donor Bill of Rights

Philanthropy is based on voluntary action for the common good. It is a tradition of giving and sharing that is primary to the quality of life. To assure that philanthropy merits the respect and trust of the general public, and that donors and prospective donors can have full confidence in the not-for-profit organizations and causes they are asked to support, we declare that all donors have these rights:

1. To be informed of the organization's mission, of the way the organization intends to use donated resources, and of its capacity to use donations effectively for their intended purposes.

2. To be informed of the identity of those serving on the organization's governing board, and to expect the board to exercise prudent judgement in its stewardship responsibilities.

3. To have access to the organization's most recent financial statements.

4. To be assured their gifts will be used for the purposes for which they were given.

5. To receive appropriate acknowledgment and recognition.

6. To be assured that information about their donations is handled with respect and with confidentiality to the extent provided by the law.

7. To expect that all relationships with individuals representing organizations of interest to the donor will be professional in nature.

8. To be informed whether those seeking donations are volunteers, employees of the organization or hired solicitors.

9. To have the opportunity to have their names deleted from mailing lists that an organization may intend to share.

10. To feel free to ask questions when making a donation and to receive prompt, truthful and forthright answers.

The text of this statement in its entirety was developed by the American Association of Fund-Raising Counsel (AAFRC), Association for Healthcare Philanthropy (AHP), Council for Advancement and Support of Education (CASE), and the Association of Fundraising (AFP), and adopted in November 1993.

Donation Stewardship Outlined in Policy

Donors, rest assured. The University of Notre Dame (Notre Dame, IN) leaves no question about donation stewardship. That's because for more than 12 years, the university has used a policy that defines its rules of conduct regarding the donations it receives.

"Our obligation policy publicly shares our commitment to university donors," says Katherine Graham, senior director of development marketing, communications and stewardship. "They are more than guidelines; they are ethical statements regarding accountability."

The seven rules discuss issues such as acknowledgment, recognition, donation usage and impact reporting. The university shares its policy (shown below) online and in its annual stewardship report.

"We are blessed with loyal alumni, parents and friends who trust university leaders to use their gifts wisely and for the intention of the donor," Graham says. "Our Obligations of Stewardship confirm this mutual trust in writing."

When creating such a policy, Graham says to keep the list of guidelines short, use simple language and share the policy with as many audiences as possible.

Source: Katherine Graham, Senior Director of Development Marketing, Communications and Stewardship, University of Notre Dame, Department of Development, Notre Dame, IN. Phone (574) 631-9785. E-mail: katherine.graham@nd.edu

Development staff with the University of Notre Dame (Notre Dame, IN) follow this series of guidelines outlined in the university policy, The Obligations of Stewardship.

The Obligations of Stewardship, University of Notre Dame (Notre Dame, IN)

As a reminder of our obligation to effectively steward contributions made to Notre Dame, the university adheres to the following guidelines:

- All gifts should be acknowledged in a timely and personal manner.
- A contribution accepted with a restricted purpose must be used for that purpose.
- If the university finds itself unable to utilize a contribution for its stated purpose, this should be communicated with the donor so that an alternative usage can be arranged.
- Whenever feasible, and especially with endowment gifts, annual impact reports should be given to the donor.
- Proper recognition should always be given to the benefactor and public recognition must be approved by the donor.
- The value of any substantial benefits as a result of contributions must be reported to each contributor.
- Contributions will be accounted for using generally accepted accounting principles, which will provide a consistent, timely and accurate reporting of all gifts into the university's official financial record.

Thank you for your enduring support of the University of Notre Dame.

Ask Donors How They Prefer You to List Their Names

For most nonprofits, not a year goes by without one or more donors' names being listed incorrectly — a spouse's name is inadvertently omitted, a name is spelled incorrectly, etc. And as embarrassing as those mistakes can be, they can occur even after demonstrating painstaking attention to detail.

With a safety net in place, however, mistakes can be dramatically minimized.

One of the wisest steps you can take is to ask donors, at the time of their pledge or gift, how they would like their names to appear when an upcoming list of contributors is published. Include that statement on all pledge forms. That way, you will have a written record of their wishes on hand.

Be Proactive in Snuffing Out Any Ill Feelings

Whenever you sense that something's wrong with a prospect or donor, it's best to address it at that time rather than avoiding it. Listening is important. What is said and how it is said should give you clues as to how best to address the issue. You may find that asking an open-ended question will give additional insight into the individual's thoughts. Also, if the individual makes a negative statement that in and of itself doesn't explain why he/she might be dissatisfied, use the technique of repeating the statement back to the individual to help gain more information:

Donor: "I don't think your organization has done a very good job."

Development Officer: "I hear you saying you're displeased with the way something has been handled in the past. Can you tell me more?"

Don't allow ill feelings to fester. Time only makes them worse. Find out what's wrong and initiate steps to resolve the problem before it's too late.

Get the Facts When a Donor Is Treated Poorly

There are many ways a donor or prospective supporter of your organization can be treated poorly by one of your own staff members, or even by another donor or volunteer.

Perhaps they called to ask for information and were put on hold for a long time or were told to call back because no one had time to help them. They may have purchased a patron table for one of your gala events, then were made the butt of a tasteless joke by the master of ceremonies.

But if you are fortunate enough to find out about the injured donor's feelings, you have an opportunity to correct the situation and salvage the relationship.

While each incident will be unique, some of these guidelines may apply to your situation, and may give you further ideas on how to apologize or make amends:

- **Thoroughly research exactly what happened.** Did anyone else in the office hear the conversation when your staff intern told a donor no one had time to help him or her, then abruptly hung up? Be sure you are aware of any special circumstances before determining your course of action.

- **Speak to the offending party first.** If the person who was unkind to your donor is from outside of your organization's jurisdiction, consider the appropriateness of contacting that person to advise him/her of the offending actions and subsequent difficulty for you. Explain why the donor felt bad — the offending party may not have been aware that his/her remarks or actions were interpreted as hurtful. Once aware, the individual may want to contact your donor personally to apologize.

- **Consider the injured party's personality.** Is he/she especially sensitive? Does even the most innocent of comments easily offend him/her? Does he/she sometimes make hurtful remarks and then bristle when someone else makes them? Even if you know the person will get over it, tell him/her you are sorry that his/her feelings were hurt. Then let it go.

- **How serious was the mistreatment?** Think of your organization as a business and your donor as the customer. What happened to the donor? Who within your organization caused the difficulty? What kind of disciplinary action is necessary? Ask the donor what you can do to make things right again. That's what good businesses do when they know a valued customer is, rightly, unhappy.

- **What kind of apology is appropriate?** Is a sincere, hand-written note from your CEO in order? Will a sympathetic phone call be enough? Invite the donor for an informal lunch, your treat, where you can visit and get to know each other better and speak in a social, relaxed atmosphere.

- **Know when to stop apologizing.** Once you have made a phone call, written a brief note, taken appropriate disciplinary action with the offending party and are satisfied that the offended donor is appeased, allow the relationship to resume normalcy.

- **Recognize when your involvement is needed, and when it's not.** There are circumstances when you may need to be a third-party diplomat between a donor and someone in your organization who has offended him/her. But before you jump in, try to learn if the two individuals already have a history together — is it longer than your history with either of them? Count to 10 before getting involved.

- **Take swift action when you can.** If one of your new or existing donors was insulted or mistreated publicly, be sure to tell him/her immediately that you are very sorry about the incident, and you plan to take appropriate action within 24 hours. Send the clear message that rudeness, insensitivity and unkindness have no place in your organization, no matter the source.

Finally, remember that you can't win them all. If you are certain that you took every reasonable action to heal the hurt feelings or indignation of one of your donors, and acted in a timely manner to correct the situation, know you did your best. Then move on.

STEWARDSHIP PROTOCOL AND ETHICS

Correct Mistakes Promptly and Without Reservation

A donor phones your office to inform you he just received an appeal addressed to him and his wife. Problem is, his wife has been deceased for six months.

A $1,000 donor writes to you and asks why she wasn't invited to the annual President's Circle reception (which includes $1,000-and-above gifts).

These are just two of the many ways an innocent mistake can cause a major rift in your relationship with your important donors. So how do you minimize the damage?

The worst thing you can do is to avoid a mistake and hope it will go away. Rather, begin by acknowledging the error and apologizing, preferably face to face. If that isn't possible, handwrite a letter of apology.

Whatever way you communicate your apology, avoid making excuses. Instead, explain how you are taking steps to see that a similar problem never occurs again. To this end,

don't hesitate to get input from the donor on how things could have or should have been done differently.

If there is a way to help compensate for the mistake, do it. Provide two free tickets to an upcoming event. Send a small plant with a note thanking the donor for bringing the matter to your attention.

Take immediate steps to avoid having a similar problem take place again. Meet with appropriate staff to discuss the matter. Create a tickler system as a reminder to check the status of the issue several weeks or months down the road.

Don't hesitate to explain to the donor — at some later date — what you have done to fix the problem. Use the opportunity to once again thank the individual for bringing it to your attention and allowing you to better serve him/her and your entire constituency.

Annual Report Advice

Although you no doubt make every effort to get donors' names listed and spelled correctly prior to producing your annual report, it's still a good idea to include a statement in your finished document that apologizes for any mistakes and asks that errors be reported to your office. Doing so will help avoid repeating mistakes in the future.

Is Everything Correct?

As hard as we try to get names listed and spelled correctly, mistakes do happen. We sincerely apologize if we have made an error and ask you to report it by contacting the Office of Development at (111) 111-1111. Doing so will help us not make the same mistake again. Thank you.

Support Donors Whose Finances Are Pinched

During this period of economic uncertainty, you may have major gift donors who are having difficulty making pledge payments. If that's the case at your organization, do what you can to help and support them. It's far wiser to maintain a positive long-term relationship than to jeopardize it.

It could be that timing is the issue rather than ability to pay.

If you discover or even sense that a donor may be having concern about pledge payments, consider these options:

1. Be proactive by offering to decrease the yearly amount and extending the payout period.

2. Consider breaking up yearly payments into quarterly or monthly payments.

3. Prepare a revised pledge payment agreement that skips a year and resumes payments the following year.

4. Don't overlook the possibility of suggesting the donor pay off the entire pledge to avoid any anxiety associated with subsequent years' payments.

Steps Help Cultivate Donors Who Live Far Away

Often, a nonprofit has a contingent of donors who keep the cause close in their hearts even though they may be far removed from it geographically.

How do you cultivate relationships and maintain interest with these important planned gift prospects and donors who live far from your organization: alumni, former residents of your community, chapter members and others?

To cultivate and steward long-distance supporters you may not be able to visit as often as you would prefer:

✓ **Establish a tickler system.** Send regular messages from your institution at irregular intervals. Create a monthly reminder of who should receive a phone call, birthday or anniversary card or other appropriate (but not contrived) communications.

✓ **Provide a virtual tour.** Besides offering a virtual tour of your facilities on your website, annually produce a video that can be distributed to all geographically distant prospects. Include a narrated tour of your facility and interviews with employees and those you serve. For older prospects, produce a nostalgic "I remember when" documentary.

✓ **Send "there's no place like home" reminders.** For former area residents, mail products or e-mail links of hometown items, from products produced in your region to books/periodicals with regional flavor or news clippings from your local newspaper.

✓ **Include personal notes with each planned gifts newsletter.** If you produce a quarterly planned gifts newsletter, include an occasional personal note for some of your far-away clients to personalize the mailing.

Although scheduling visits to viable planned gift prospects at least once a year is advantageous, these cultivation strategies will serve to strengthen ties with these key individuals.

Stewardship Essentials: The Donor Relations Guide.
Edited by Scott C. Stevenson.
© 2011 Stevenson, Inc. Published 2011 by Stevenson, Inc.

Stewardship Essentials: The Donor Relations Guide

ENGAGING BOARD MEMBERS AND EMPLOYEES IN STEWARDSHIP

Although one individual at your organization may be responsible for managing the stewardship program, many — fellow employees, volunteers, board members — can and should be involved in acts of stewardship with your donors. Your board members, in particular, can play a key role in stewarding your most generous donors.

Donor Recognition Idea

Have you ever considered using your organization's board meetings as a way to recognize key donors' generous gifts?

Make a point to invite recent donors to be introduced and perhaps make a brief address at each meeting. Doing so provides a special kind of donor recognition and also emphasizes the importance of principal giving among board members and staff.

Ask Employees to Help Steward Donors

Donors appreciate hearing from those who benefit from their generosity.

Encourage your nonprofit's employees whose work or departments may be positively impacted by major gifts to show their appreciation to those who made it possible. Ask that employees keep your office aware of and involved in such gestures of appreciation so as not to be left out of the communication loop.

Get Board Members to Thank Generous Contributors

Getting a note or phone call of appreciation from a board member can be impressive.

Whether your board meets monthly or quarterly, provide them with a list of contributors since the last board meeting and invite those present to write down the names and addresses of those they would be willing to write or phone with a message of appreciation. The simple but regular exercise of having board members thank your more generous contributors helps them more fully appreciate the role of philanthropy in your ongoing operations and also helps ready them for eventual solicitation calls.

Ask Employees to Demonstrate Gifts' Impact

Your organization's employees can play a key role in showing donors the impact of particular gifts: uses of equipment, newly-funded programs, endowed funds and more.

Once a donor's gift has been implemented, take time to meet on your own with departments or individual employees whose work has been impacted by the donor's gift. Ask them to demonstrate a new piece of equipment or discuss how the gift is positively influencing their work. How is the gift making their work more productive? How is it impacting those served by your organization.

Once you have a personal understanding of the gift's impact, work with that department or individual employee to create a demonstration that could be shared with the donor(s) who made the gift possible. Come up with a list of questions and answers that the employee can address when you schedule a time for the donor to stop by and meet with that department or employee.

Whenever you take the time to schedule a demonstration between a department or employee and the donor who made it all possible, you accomplish three things: 1) The donor gains a greater understanding and satisfaction of his/her gift; 2) the department or employee gains a greater understanding of what's involved with fund development; and 3) the donor gets more connected with people outside of the advancement office which serves as an additional connecting point with your organization and its work.

Examples of Employee Demonstrations

✓ **How a new piece of equipment works** — shows the donor how the purchase is making work easier, more productive and, in some instances, more cost efficient.

✓ **Newly-funded or expanded program or service** — shows the donor how you are able to enhance those services provided to patients or students or others.

✓ **Endowed nurses scholarship** — shows donors how you can serve more financially-deserving students. In this instance, you may want to include scholarship recipients in a discussion with the donor.

✓ **Endowed chair or professorship** — shows the donor the value of this position to your organization and those you serve.

✓ **Capital improvements** — a tour led by the department or employee shows the donor how this addition or newly-renovated space will allow employees to accomplish even more and how it will positively impact those you serve.

ENGAGING BOARD MEMBERS AND EMPLOYEES IN STEWARDSHIP

Hold a Thank-a-thon to Recognize Donors, Recharge Board Members

Does the thought of coordinating an organized effort to thank your many donors seem overwhelming and time consuming? Consider a Thank-a-thon, a technique that works well for Jewish Family Service of Greater Dallas (Dallas, TX).

Every two or three months, Development Director Amy Walton organizes the thank-a-thon, in which board members call donors of all gift sizes with a personal message of thanks, answer questions they have and invite them to come for a personal tour. Over two hours, five or six board members are able to make more than 200 calls, Walton says.

In an effort to stay connected with lapsed contributors, in Fall 2008 Walton had board members call donors who gave in 2006 or 2007 but had not yet given in 2008. The calls were strictly to say thanks, she says, but if the donor explicitly asks how to make a contribution, board members are able to provide options to do so.

Board member volunteers receive scripts and an information card (prepared using Microsoft Word's catalogue function under Mail Merge; see example, right) for each donor referencing family names and recent gift history that has a space to make notes about the conversation to be entered into the organization's donor software.

"Amongst the sea of direct mail, holiday cards, bills and more, we want our donors to know that they are valued by Jewish Family Service," says Walton. "And even when they have to cut back or cut out giving (as many may have to do in this economic crisis), we still consider them to be a part of our family. Personal contact makes the donor feel special and we find this kind of stewardship stands apart from the most eloquently written thank-you letter."

Board members who participate in the thank-a-thon are encouraged to attend annual fundraising training, but Walton says she always emphasizes that personal passion is all that is needed to be effective: "If they communicate why they contribute/volunteer/advocate for Jewish Family Service, it will resonate with those they interact with, whether it is a friend they see in the grocery store or a stranger they call during our thank-a-thon."

Board member Linda Garner, who has participated in three thank-a-thons, says the efforts are rewarding and reinforce her commitment to the organization. "Every single person thanks you for calling," she says. "Many of the donors I called said how nice it was to be thanked without being asked for anything in return."

Walton says not a thank-a-thon goes by without board members saying how rejuvenated they feel from the experience.

Thank-a-thons are held either before a board meeting or scheduled for a specific night. Walton says the group effort creates a more positive experience because they can feed off the positive energy of working together.

At calling sessions, volunteers meet for snacks and a brief visit, then staff do a quick orientation about the category of donors they'll be calling and how the thank-a-thon fits into the overall development cycle. Thank-a-Thon room signs are hung on doors of offices that board members can use to make calls by personal cell phone or office phone line.

Source: Amy Walton, Development Director; Robin Sachs, Board President; and Linda Garner, Board Member, Jewish Family Service, Dallas, TX. Phone (972) 437-9950, ext. 209.

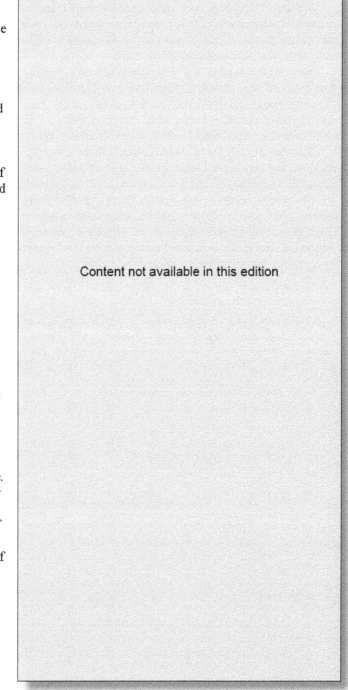

Content not available in this edition

Thank-you Calling Campaign Involves, Inspires and Educates Board Members

Board members at SHALVA (Chicago, IL) — a nonprofit that provides domestic violence counseling services to the Jewish community — regularly call donors to say thanks.

"I think it is impossible to thank donors too much for supporting SHALVA's programs, especially given the current fundraising environment," says Ava Newbart, director of development. "These simple thank-you calls are a great opportunity for SHALVA to personally connect with donors. They are also a way to inspire our board to keep fundraising and promoting SHALVA to our community."

Since SHALVA's office has only four phone lines and a small budget, Newbart asks board members to call donors on their own.

For their first calling campaign, board members called all year-end donors of $50 or more. Newbart e-mailed board members a script, call report form and a list of names with phone numbers. Each board member was asked to make an average of 20 phone calls, for a total of approximately 400 calls.

Newbart followed up with board members via e-mail, encouraging them to make their calls and send back the forms. "One board member e-mailed me back and asked, 'You want me to call, say thank you and not ask for anything else? Are you sure?'" she says. "I reassured her, and other board members, that their phone calls would be well received and that they would be happily surprised at donors' responses."

She also reminds board members that with the economy as it is, SHALVA must reach out and personally contact donors; that it's much easier to keep current donors than to find new donors; and that the need for SHALVA's services is on the rise.

For other nonprofits considering starting a simple thank-you campaign, Newbart advises: "Just do it and keep it simple. Being a one-woman shop is challenging. We've talked about making personal thank-you calls for a long time, but there were always competing priorities. Given the climate, our board was open to trying new strategies. Keeping our donors happy is an agency-wide mantra."

Source: Ava Newbart, Director of Development, SHALVA, Chicago, IL. Phone (773) 583-4673. E-mail: anewbart@shalvaonline.org

Two tools that staff with SHALVA (Chicago, IL) provide to board members to make donor thank-you calls are the call report, below, and information sheet with sample scripts, at right.

Content not available in this edition

The Conversation:
The intention of your call is ONLY to thank donors for their gifts received.

Sample Opener:
"Hello, Mr./Mrs. X. My name is Jane Brown and I'm a member of the volunteer board of directors of SHALVA. I am calling to thank you for your support of our organization. We received your recent gift and I wanted to let you know, personally, how very much we appreciate it."

At this point, simply pause and wait for a response. Some donors are quite startled and don't know what to say. Usually, they are very appreciative and gracious.

Most calls are very short, simply ending after you express your thanks. **Please do NOT make any comment that could be construed as another request,** such as "We are grateful for your gift and hope you will continue to support us in the future." This hints of another solicitation, and we want to avoid leaving that impression.

Sample Closer:
You can end the call by simply wishing the donor a pleasant evening.

Sometimes a caller will ask you about how SHALVA is doing or will want some information about our programs and services. If you are comfortable answering their questions, by all means do so. If not, perhaps you could ask if they would like a staff member to contact them separately. If so, please let us know. If a donor expresses an interest in giving more or in volunteering time, you can definitely engage in that discussion. Other organizations' experience with thank-you calls by board members has shown that a small number of donors want to discuss making an additional gift and sometimes it can be significantly higher than the gift they have recently made.

What happens as a result of these calls?
Donors who receive a personal call (including those who received messages left on answering machines) will be specially coded by the office, and any additional information gathered during the calls will also be recorded.

The next time these donors are solicited along with other donors who did not receive a call, we will be able to compare their average gift levels, their rate of response, the promptness of response and other information. We can continue to compare these groups for a couple of years, which will allow us to measure long-term loyalty of the two groups. Though we anticipate that donors who receive personal calls are likely to show greater loyalty over time and make increasingly generous gifts, we need reliable information from this test for future planning and forecasting.

Stewardship Essentials: The Donor Relations Guide

STEWARDING CAPITAL CAMPAIGN DONORS

The ways in which you steward those who have made "bricks and mortar" contributions may vary from those making other types of gifts. Following are some tips and examples of how to steward those who support your capital fundraising efforts.

Share Construction Updates With Donors, Would-be Donors

During the construction of a new student residence and dining commons at Bates College (Lewiston, ME), Doug Hubley of the college's office of communications and media relations wrote regular updates on the progress of the construction.

To share Hubley's observations, staff posted his construction updates on the college's news home page (www.bates.edu/x165427.xml) at least once a month throughout the construction that began in 2006 and ended in 2008, sometimes more frequently if developments warranted, says Bryan McNulty, director of communications and media relations.

A campus construction update also served as an anchored feature in every BatesNews, a monthly e-newsletter sent to about 21,000 alumni, parents and friends, and copied to all faculty and staff.

"These updates became popular with readers," says McNulty. "Doug wrote them with his own voice and developed a following of folks who looked forward both to his information and wry humor in photo captions and salted through the text."

The goals of the campus construction updates, McNulty says, were to:

✓ Generate interest and excitement in the college's major physical improvements (a key message).

✓ Show how the construction relates to a campus facilities master plan. Message: Bates is a strategic and careful steward.

✓ Engage with alumni, potential donors.

✓ Keep the campus community in the know on developments related to the college's major construction projects.

To encourage engagement, Hubley ended each update with the following line, which helped elicit queries and comments: "Can we talk? What do you think about the campus improvements process? What do you know that we don't? We want to hear from you. Please e-mail your questions and comments to: Doug Hubley (link to his e-mail address) with 'Construction Update' in the subject line."

Check out an online archive of Hubley's campus construction updates at:
www.bates.edu/campus-improvements.xml

Source: Bryan McNulty, Director, Communications and Media Relations, Bates College, Lewiston, ME. Phone (207) 786-6330. E-mail: bmcnulty@bates.edu

Include Donors in Post-campaign Success

Just because your capital campaign has successfully concluded doesn't mean the party's over. It's important to share your campaign's success with donors. After all, their generosity made it a success.

Involve donors in your post-campaign period in the following ways:

• Convey appreciation in a personal way through various methods: personal letters from your organization's CEO, campaign chair and others.

• Follow through on naming gifts with appropriate plaques. Check with donors to be sure names are spelled and listed correctly before authorizing the engraving.

• Invite donors to celebrate in the completion of renovated or newly constructed capital projects to which they contributed. Consider a larger, all-inclusive celebration as well as more individualized gatherings.

• For donors who establish named endowment funds, revisit the details of the fund: how annual interest will be used, the agreed-to name and fund description and such.

Engage Major Donors With Capital Project Scrapbook

Looking for a way to steward your capital project donors? Laurie Rogers, director of development, Peter Paul Development Center (Richmond, VA), suggests starting a scrapbook of your building's progress.

Rogers has created a photo scrapbook for the last three capital projects she has been involved with in Richmond. At the groundbreaking, she presents donors with a three-ring binder. She then mails photo updates to them — already three-hole punched — at least once a month.

"I include a note about how things are going," says Rogers. "In this economy, any progress is good progress." Donors unable to attend the groundbreaking receive the binder by mail or a personal delivery.

Rogers suggests scheduling hardhat tours once a quarter for donors to see the progress for themselves: "Even if they don't come to campus, they know that you are tending this investment that they have so graciously and generously made in your project," she says. "In all three capital projects I've been involved in, the message has always been the same — gratitude. The donors have been quite appreciative of this effort."

Source: Laurie Rogers, Director of Development, Peter Paul Development Center, Richmond, VA. Phone (804) 780-1195. E-mail: plrogers@earthlink.net

Why and How to Say Thanks Following Your Major Capital Campaign

Your capital campaign is over, and it's a great success. Your volunteers and staff members are ready to breathe a sigh of relief, put their feet up and bask in the glow of a job well done.

Don't rest on your laurels. Rather, jump on the momentum to reach out to your donors and tell them those all-important two words: thank you.

Swarthmore College (Swarthmore, PA) raised more than $245 million during the most ambitious and successful campaign in its history. To show how important the campaign has been to Swarthmore, and to let some of the people who benefited say thank you, they created a 10-minute online video to be screened at a series of seven regional post-campaign celebrations.

Video Highlights

The video highlighted the direct outcomes of the campaign, including curricular and academic enhancements, new and renovated facilities, financial aid and student life initiatives. Interspersed within each of these elements, and at the end of the video, were direct thank yous by Swarthmore College students, faculty, staff and board members.

"While some of our board spokespeople are exceptionally generous to the college, we didn't choose them because of this," says Patricia A. Laws, director of alumni development. "Instead, we chose a wider cross-section of constituents who could help tell the campaign's story in a meaningful, personal way."

The donor events (and the video programming for them) were suggested and conceptualized by campaign leadership at a meeting of the college's development and communications committee, a standing committee of the college's board of managers, says Laws.

The video was produced by the same vendor that produced the college's campaign announcement video.

"We are also fortunate to have a special projects director in the president's office who has a background in television production and she really helped complete the project on very tight time frames," she says.

The celebration events attracted about 1,000 people.

"Those who viewed the film in the company of other Swarthmoreans had the strongest and most favorable reactions, and quite a few requested copies to send along to friends and classmates," says Laws.

Video Distribution and Response

After the final event, several hundred top campaign donors and volunteers received a DVD copy with a note of thanks from the college's president. Traveling development staff also distributed copies, and the disks were made widely available on campus. It was also posted as a progressive download on the college's website.

"The video was a good addition to our campaign stewardship plans, which included a 96-page report showing tangible outcomes and listing all 23,000 campaign donors. It was mailed to the entire constituency, and we had a series of countdown and results e-mails that reached a high percentage of alumni," she says. "The video on our website complemented each of these, and provided another opportunity to reinforce the importance of every donor's gift."

Donors who received copies by mail also continue to compliment the piece, says Laws: "This suggests that it may have taken a while for the disks to make the 'long trip from the mailbox' to a computer or DVD player."

Source: Patricia A. Laws, CFRE, Director of Alumni Development, Swarthmore College, Swarthmore, PA. Phone (800) 525-8622. E-mail: plaws1@swarthmore.edu

Stewardship Essentials: The Donor Relations Guide

STEWARDING ENDOWMENT DONORS

Just as the methods used to steward capital campaign donors have unique approaches, the same is true of donors who support your endowment. Because a named endowment gift should benefit those you serve for generations to come, there are many and unique ways in which you can demonstrate the impact of such gifts.

Steward Those Who Have Established Endowed Gifts

Do you provide a formal yearly update to persons who have established endowed funds with your organization? Informing these donors of their fund's status and impact should be a must for two reasons: It's a good stewardship practice and doing so could very easily lead to donors adding more to established funds.

Meet one-on-one with those who have set up endowed funds to:

1. **Review the current progress of your organization's overall endowment for the past year.** Who is managing your endowment? Did the fund grow? At what rate? Were there any changes in your endowment's investment policy?

2. **Review the individual's established endowment fund.** What was the amount of annual interest used to underwrite the program for which the fund was established? What rate of return was made available and how was it calculated?

3. **How were the funds used?** If the endowed fund was a scholarship, for instance, who were the recipients and how much did each receive? Give the donor a solid sense of how the gift is having a positive impact on those you serve.

4. **Help the donor extend his/her understanding of the endowed fund to a higher level.** Paint a picture of what more could be accomplished were more funds added to the endowment, either through outright gifts, a planned gift or both. Do so in a way, however, that doesn't undercut what has already been contributed.

5. **Leave the donor with a written summary of your presentation.** Give him/her a document to review.

This formal update and stewardship procedure will make the donor more aware that his/her fund is a living gift that continues to impact your cause yearly.

Host an Annual Event to Thank Endowment Donors

Just as you might host an annual event to thank all contributors at the $1,000-and-above level, consider hosting a similar event geared to the past year's endowment donors, assuming you have sufficient numbers to merit such an event. An endowment dinner or reception draws attention to the importance of building your endowment and also recognizes these important contributors.

You can use your event to:

- Point out endowment performance for the past year.
- Provide attendees with a printed handout that describes all named endowment funds and who supported each for the past year.
- Announce newly established endowment funds.
- Showcase the impact particular funds have on your nonprofit organization and the lives of those you serve.
- Generate publicity about your endowment by selectively inviting key media officials.
- Make special note of realized planned gifts for that year which have been earmarked for endowment purposes.

Thoroughly Acknowledge Endowment Gifts

Whenever an endowment gift is made, it's important to acknowledge the donor's investment thoroughly. A letter of thanks is not enough. The acknowledgment should include an update on the status of the named fund and general comments about your organization's endowment:

- How the fund's annual proceeds have been used during the past year.
- The impact of the fund on programs and/or services — how it is making a difference.
- The principle total within the donor's named endowed fund.
- The annual rate of return (interest rate and dollar amount).
- The total amount and health of your organization's endowment.
- A comment about the investment committee and its investment philosophy.

A thorough update on each endowment gift helps to keep the fund a living, viable gift that continues to fulfill its intended purpose and to motivate future gifts.

STEWARDING ENDOWMENT DONORS

Marketing Endowments Starts With Stewarding Existing Funds

To successfully market your endowment, you need to know and understand what you are marketing and be able to illustrate that understanding to your donor prospects, says J. Richard Ely, Jr., owner of Strategic Fundraising Consultants (Providence, RI).

One of the most effective ways to do so, Ely says, is to work with your board members, chief financial officer, investment committees and others within your organization to create a one-page description of your endowment.

Your endowment description should include:

- A breakdown of the asset allocation in your endowment (stocks, bonds, cash), the amount of each and the grand total.

- A performance analysis that shows how your endowment's assets performed compared to industry averages over time.

- A breakdown of restrictions on the endowment — (e.g., permanently and temporarily restricted and unrestricted).

- The primary investment objective of your endowment, which is based on your endowment's investment policy.

- Who internally is responsible for endowment management — typically, your investment committee and their professional affiliations.

- Who manages your endowment investments, if you have an outside firm.

- The endowment investments custodian — who holds the assets, processes the buy and sell orders, collects income and prepares statements.

"The endowment description shows prospects that you know what you're doing, that you are going to manage their fund into perpetuity, and that you are responsible enough to do that," says Ely.

As a companion piece to your endowment description, it's important to include a list all of your endowment funds that shows donor prospects you have a long history of careful management of named endowment funds, he says.

"The objection I hear the most from endowment donors is, 'If I give you the money, how do I know it will be used for the purpose I intend it for 50 years from now'," says Ely. "When donor prospects see an endowment fund on your list that was established in 1922 to purchase science books for your library, for example, and that you are still doing that every year, they will feel confident that if they give you their money, you will do the same for them."

With an endowment description and current endowment list in hand, you can begin to look at all the ways

Content not available in this edition

Tools that help you successfully market your endowment include an Endowment Description, immediately above, which shows prospects how you will manage their money; and a list of existing endowments, top, which illustrates that others have entrusted you with their gifts, and how you are responsibly managing those gifts.

you can publicize your endowment, says Ely. Ways to do so include feature stories in your newsletter that showcase donors and recipients and talk about the benefits of endowment and a listing of all endowment funds in your annual report. He also recommends holding an annual event that showcases your endowment and its donors.

*Source: J. Richard Ely, Jr., Owner, Strategic Fundraising Consultants, Providence, RI. Phone (401) 274-3863.
E-mail: rely@planned-giving.com*

STEWARDING ENDOWMENT DONORS

Focus on the Positive When Sharing Endowment Returns

While economic downturns have negatively impacted endowment funds at the Akron Community Foundation (Akron, OH), the foundation's prudent financial policy has helped lessen that impact — which is the message foundation officials are communicating to donors, says Suzanne Allen, vice president for development.

"Our funds operate on a 12-quarter rolling average, which works out the highs and lows of the market," Allen says. "As a result, donors generally always have income in their funds to disperse."

Rather than drawing attention to the decrease in endowment fund value, Allen says they have chosen to emphasize how their conservative investment policy has kept all of their endowment funds from going underwater. Donors were also very philanthropic during the economic downturn, she says.

They are distributing this message in the foundation's quarterly newsletter, in the foundation's annual report, and at public speaking engagements by senior staff.

A letter in the annual report co-authored by the board chair and president states: "Our board's adherence to our prudent financial policy resulted in the foundation remaining fully invested in the public investment markets, which led to a 34 percent increase in the market value of our assets. This helped maintain grant-making levels when community needs were highest, benefiting local agencies that rely on Akron Community Foundation endowments for financial support. It also helped fund the key initiatives and other grants you will read about in this report."

In his foundation newsletter message, Foundation President John H. Petures, Jr., said: "This is an exciting time for our organization and our investors. We finished the fiscal year on March 31, 2010, with a 34 percent net investment return for the previous 12-month period, a remarkable turnaround given the incredible economic upheaval we all experienced during the past 18 months. Guided by prudent investment policy and boosted by the generosity of our donors, Akron Community Foundation's endowment has grown to more than $126 million."

In addition to the president's message, the newsletter contained an article focusing on the 34 percent increase in the foundation's endowment.

Source: Suzanne Allen, Vice President, Development, Akron Community Foundation, Akron, OH. Phone (330) 376-8522. E-mail: sallen@akroncommunityfdn.org

This excerpt from the annual report for the Akron Community Foundation (Akron, OH) shows how development officials communicated the value of its long-standing prudent investment policy.

Content not available in this edition

Design an Endowment Donors Display

A visible display of endowment donors' names can both encourage persons to give to endowment and recognize those who have already done so.

Whether it's a donor wall, kiosk or other display, showcase names of those who have made named endowment gifts (at a set minimum requirement) at a highly visible location on your premises (e.g., main lobby, reception area, lounge). Arrange names by year in which funds were established so names can be added in years to come.

Having an endowment-only donor display gives prominence to endowment gifts and encourages passersby to consider the possibility of establishing similar gifts.

STEWARDING ENDOWMENT DONORS

Communicate With Donors About 'Underwater' Endowments

Keeping major donors in the communications loop — even when the news is less than positive — is an important part of donor relations.

In February 2009, staff with Kent State University (Kent, OH) sent letters to 410 endowment donors informing them how the economy had impacted their endowments.

The letters, each hand-signed by the executive director of the Kent State University Foundation, were created from a template and personalized for each donor to include the name of the donor's endowment fund and its market value as of Dec. 31, 2008, as well as how much it had decreased since July 1, 2008.

"The third paragraph of the letter was also personalized based on the wording of each agreement and whether or not the scholarship was underwater (market value is less than its historic dollar value) after the downturn in the economic market," says Scott McKinney, associate director of stewardship. "We did not ask them to allow us to invade the principal, but have allowed amendments to the endowments if requested."

Seven donors requested that university officials amend their agreements to allow invasion of the principal, McKinney says, and two donors have requested that the university amend their agreements to not allow invasion of the principal. Seven donors have made additional gifts to ensure that their scholarship is awarded next year.

"We have received many positive comments from our donors about this letter," McKinney notes. "They seemed to appreciate our transparency, even though the news was less than positive."

Source: Scott McKinney, Associate Director, Stewardship, Institutional Advancement, Kent State University, Kent, OH. Phone (330) 672-0347. E-mail: smckinne@kent.edu

Content not available in this edition

Officials from Kent State University (Kent, OH) share the template for a personalized letter informing endowment donors how the economy has impacted their endowments.

STEWARDING ENDOWMENT DONORS

Proper Stewardship Expands List of Donors

Augustana College (Rock Island, IL) has 790 endowment funds totaling $88.2 million. Thirty-nine of them are general funds, and the rest have restrictions designed for scholarships, programs or chairs (see full list at www.augustana. edu/giving/endowment).

Endowed scholarships start at $25,000. An endowed faculty chair can be named for $1.5 million. The cost to endow an Academic Venture Fund, which encourages entrepreneurial thinking among faculty, is $250,000.

Anne Bergren, director of donor relations and stewardship, credits the successful endowment program to its engaged alumni base and history of careful stewardship of endowed funds. "We have donors who have funded several endowments because they found our stewardship of their gifts so meaningful," she says.

That careful stewardship includes:

- Annual reports to donors or succeeding family members.

- Personal notes from students (for scholarship donors).

- Invitations to events and lectures.

- Letters from faculty members expressing their gratitude for a gift.

- Communication with scholarship donors about their students' successes, which causes them to feel an affinity to their students.

The majority of Augustana's restricted endowments are scholarships. To help connect scholarship students to their endowed scholarship donors, Bergren says, they share donor stories with each scholarship student. These printed donor stories, written by donors and/or their families, illustrate why they endowed the scholarship.

"Most graduates from Augustana benefited from scholarship assistance," says Bergren. "That's why most alumni feel very strongly about establishing an endowed scholarship. They do it as a way of giving back."

Source: Anne E. Bergren, Director of Donor Relations & Stewardship, Augustana College, Rock Island, IL. Phone (309) 794-7228. E-mail: annebergren@augustana.edu

Stewardship Essentials: The Donor Relations Guide

STEWARDING PLANNED GIFT AND MEMORIAL GIFT DONORS

How can you properly steward those donors whose gifts may not be fully realized until after their lifetimes? What can you do to express gratitude and attempt to share the impact of their unrealized gifts? There are a number of ways in which you can steward these special donors throughout their lifetimes.

Six Ways to Steward Your Bequest Donors

Bequest donors should be acknowledged and recognized, says Janet L. Hedrick, senior associate, Bentz Whaley Flessner (Arlington, VA). "Bequest donors should be treated like major donors during their lifetime and should not be forgotten once they pass away," she insists.

Hedrick shares six ways to steward your bequest donors:

1. Hold an annual luncheon event that older attendees can more easily attend. The speaker should be a student, faculty member or client who benefited from bequests received in the past.

2. Quantify funds established by bequest or planned gifts, including the number of students, faculty or clients deriving benefit from those funds. Feature these results in your annual membership updates.

3. Send birthday cards to bequest donors.

4. Pay personal visits to bequest donors.

5. Include their names in publications.

6. Create a special tie for male donors and a scarf for female planned giving society members.

Source: Janet L. Hedrick, CFRE, Sr. Associate, Bentz Whaley Flessner, Arlington, VA. Phone (703) 413-5505.
E-mail: jhedrick@bwf.com

A Look Into Stewarding Bequest Donors

Bequests are revocable planned gifts. Steward your bequest donors to show you are thinking of them and to encourage annual/major support during their lifetime.

Here are three ways to steward bequest donors:

"All endowed fund donors to the Wake Forest University School of Medicine sign official fund agreements. Thus, when a donor has a planned gift that will eventually endow a fund, we honor the donor on the anniversary date of his/her signature on the fund agreement. Our anniversary stewardship reports note, 'This month marks the six-year anniversary of your signature on the John Smith Scholarship Fund Agreement, and we remain deeply grateful for your support. One day your benevolent fund will support XYZ, and here are some of the recent initiatives and breakthroughs currently happening in...'

"We enclose meaningful news, updates, press releases, etc. that focus on the area/department that will eventually benefit from the donor's planned gift. This lets the donor know we are thinking of them and we hope they are thinking of us."

— Erika A. Friedel, Director of Donor Relations,
Office of Development & Alumni Affairs, Wake Forest University
Baptist Medical Center (Winston-Salem, NC)

"For our bequest donors, we hold an annual luncheon. This year we scheduled the luncheon to follow a symphony performance on our campus, which we also invited them to attend. At the luncheon following, we gave each guest a bud vase with our logo (with roses in them — which also served as the centerpiece for each table). Most importantly, for those who could not attend, we sent the vase with candy and a note telling them they were missed, to which we received many kind responses. This way we were able to reach each member of our bequest society."

— Susan Burr Williams, Institutional Advancement,
Saint Joseph College (West Hartford, CT)

"We host an annual luncheon to honor our society members who have established scholarships or made bequests to Cummings School of Veterinary Medicine in their will. We usually have a few students and faculty give testimonials emphasizing how the bequest/scholarship made their veterinary education possible. This is not a fancy or expensive event. We receive overwhelming positive feedback each year and it's a good way to teach our students and staff about stewardship as well."

— Elizabeth Stearns, Director Annual Giving,
Cummings School of Veterinary Medicine (Grafton, MA)

Acknowledge Donors in Unique Ways

 What unique ways are you acknowledging your planned giving donors?

"One of the member benefits for our Benedictine Legacy Society is a Saint John's Estate Planning Binder. This binder has an embossed cover showing our Abbey Church, a major architectural touch point. It has plastic sleeves for holding documents related to a donor's estate plans, such as trust documents, will, advisor's contact information, etc. Each section has a log for noting the latest information additions.

"Some donors use it as the basic storage for their papers and keep it in a secure location. Others put photocopies of documents in the sleeves with notes describing the location of the original documents. We very strongly recommend that originals be placed in safety deposit boxes or other secure locations.

"Many donors have expressed appreciation for the usefulness of the book in two ways: It reminds them of what documents are important and also provides a copy of the documents for heirs to use to identify originals."

— Jim Dwyer, Director of Planned Giving,
Saint John's University and Abbey (Collegeville, MN)

Prioritize Uses for Unrestricted Bequests

What happens when your organization is surprised with a six-figure bequest that has no strings attached? Do you use it for general operations? Do you earmark it for your general endowment?

Create and prioritize a top-10 list of ways you would earmark unrestricted bequests. That way you will be prepared to use both expected and unexpected funds in the most thoughtful and prudent way. And by all means, avoid using bequests to underwrite general operations. Doing so sends the wrong message to those who might consider future bequests.

Beyond a top-10 list, be sure that you also have on hand a board-approved planned gifts policy addressing any number of issues related to marketing, establishing, accepting and stewarding planned gifts. Use the box, right, as a checklist to review or create such a gifts policy.

> **Planned Gifts Policies**
>
> A board-approved planned gifts policy should address issues including but not limited to:
>
> - Ethics Statement
> - Definitions/Terminology
> - Duties and Responsibilities
> - Instrument Guidelines
> - Establishment Procedures
> - Gift Acceptance and Approval Procedures
> - Gift Acknowledgment
> - Recognition/Stewardship
> - Confidentiality Information

Host an Annual Memorial Event for Employees, Constituents

To honor the memory of those close to your organization — donors, volunteers, employees, board members and others — why not host an annual memorial event that recognizes those who have died during the past year?

Invite loved ones of persons who have passed away, as well as the public, to an hour-long service that pays tribute to persons who had a connection to your organization.

Such an annual service might include:

✓ Asking the family and friends of each individual to stand and be recognized.

✓ A printed program listing those who have died during the past year along with a brief bio of their lives and affiliation with your organization.

✓ A permanent wall display or memorial book to honor those who have been memorialized in past years.

An annual service such as this shows respect for these individuals' contributions and emphasizes the fact that they were an important part of your nonprofit's extended family.

Encourage the Living by Remembering the Deceased

Show the living how the memory of deceased benefactors — those who have remembered your charity through their estates — is being kept alive.

Your ongoing acts of stewardship for those no longer living will serve to encourage others to make planned gifts as well.

Ways to pay tribute to deceased benefactors may include:

- Names on buildings, offices, engraved brick walkways/walls.

- Names on endowed funds or ongoing programs.

- Names associated with annual awards: notable friends/donors, annual stipends to outstanding employees or those served by your agency and more.

- Feature articles in your publications that point out the deceased's legacy to your charity and those you serve.

- An annual listing of all (the deceased included) planned gift donors.

- An annual memorial service recognizing deceased benefactors.

Take Memorial Gifts a Step Further

Many nonprofits gladly accept memorial gifts, but that's often where the relationship ends — with a onetime gift. The sole opportunity that presented itself to establish a relationship with all those who made a contribution ends as soon as it began. Depending on the number of memorial gifts your charity receives, there could be a number of opportunities to establish a relationship with those who make a contribution in memory of someone.

To build a relationship with memorial contributors, take these actions:

1. Have a sound gift acknowledgment procedure in place. In addition to thanking each contributor in a personal way, provide to the deceased's family the list of contributors, along with amounts and addresses.

2. Be sure to add all names to your mailing list.

3. List the names of the deceased (in bold) in your annual roll of contributors along with the names of each who contributed in their memory.

4. Host a memorial service once a year at your facility — inviting all those who made memorial contributions — to remember those who died that year. Use the occasion to cultivate relationships with those who attend and provide tours of your facilities.

5. Produce a memorial book that is displayed and contains the names and dates of all who have been memorialized at your organization.

6. For memorial gifts that collectively amount to a sizeable sum, meet with the family to discuss ways the funds might be used, including the establishment of a named endowed fund that the family could add to over time.

Stewardship Essentials: The Donor Relations Guide

CORRESPONDENCE, PRINTED COMMUNICATIONS THAT SUPPORT STEWARDSHIP EFFORTS

Although face-to-face communication is by far the most genuine and effective way of stewarding donors, correspondence and printed materials can help to underscore those efforts in countless ways. This chapter shares examples of how correspondence and printed materials support your stewardship efforts.

Regularly Change, Update Letters of Gift Acknowledgment

No one likes receiving a form letter in thanks for a gift they have made.

The minute a donor picks up on the fact that the letter was generated by a computer program and not personally penned with their specific gift in mind, the letter loses its meaning and gets discarded. And yet, when you're sending dozens of gift acknowledgment letters regularly, it's difficult to personalize every one of them.

To keep gift acknowledgment letters fresh and as personal as possible, create two or three different letters from which you can draw, depending on the gift amount and to whom it is directed. In addition, include room for not one, but at least two paragraphs that are personal in nature. A portion of the letter can be standardized, but more than the person's name and gift amount can be personalized.

Finally, be sure to add a postscript (P.S.) after signing the letter as one more step that makes it a truly personalized thank you.

Below is a sample gift acknowledgment letter that illustrates the combination of personal and standardized messages.

This example of a gift acknowledgment letter includes personal information in the first and last paragraphs, along with a handwritten P.S., all of which add to its uniqueness — and appeal — from the recipient's perspective.

Haven House

PO Box 3029 • Lafferty, WY 83110

Dear Sarah and John:

Thank you so much for the recent gift of $500 to be used to enhance our career development program. Your ongoing loyalty to Haven House is so very much appreciated by our employees, our board and those we serve on a daily basis.

I'm pleased to report that during the past several months we have been able to make some noticeable achievements:

- A $50,000 grant was received to continue outreach efforts to rural communities in a three-county area.

- Our career development efforts have allowed us to find employment for 31 clients who are making the transition to being on their own for the first time. That's a nine percent increase over last year's efforts.

- Due to several new partnerships with both government agencies and partnering businesses, we have a much more coordinated effort in place to identify individuals in need of our services and come to their aid immediately.

I would invite both of you to stop by for a visit and tour when your time permits. I'd love to show you some of what's happening here. I remember your telling me last time we talked that you were traveling to New England. I would enjoy hearing about your trip.

Again, thank you for investing in Haven House.

Sincerely,

Betty Alman

Betty Alman
Executive Director

P.S. Thanks again! Please say hi to your children from me. -B

Letter Serves as Stewardship, Cultivation Tool

In light of today's economy, it's becoming increasingly important to talk about your institution's mission and those it serves, says Kenneth L. Converse, vice president for institutional advancement, Buena Vista University (Storm Lake, IA): "We need to do a better job of communicating with our donors about how we are using their dollars."

With this in mind, Converse and his staff recently sent a letter to the 419 donors who made gifts in 2003 to the university's Estelle Siebens Science Center. Signed by the dean of the School of Science, the letter (shown below) thanked donors for their support and highlighted the program's successes.

"We wanted our donors to feel good about what they did," Converse says. "We wrestled with length, but our sense was that those who were interested in reading the letter would get the powerful message we were trying to convey about the impact the new building has had on our students and institution."

This was the first time they had sent a stewardship letter for anything other than an endowed fund, says Converse, who notes he and his staff plan to look at how they might use this stewardship and cultivation strategy with other projects.

"We should have sent the letter sooner, and would have had we thought about it," he admits. "As it was, the timing was about a year off, but the letter was sent out after our first group of students had finished their four years in the program. Everyone on the recipient list had completed their pledge payments."

Source: Kenneth L. Converse, Vice President for Institutional Advancement, Buena Vista University, Storm Lake, IA. Phone (712) 749-2101. E-mail: CONVERSEK@bvu.edu

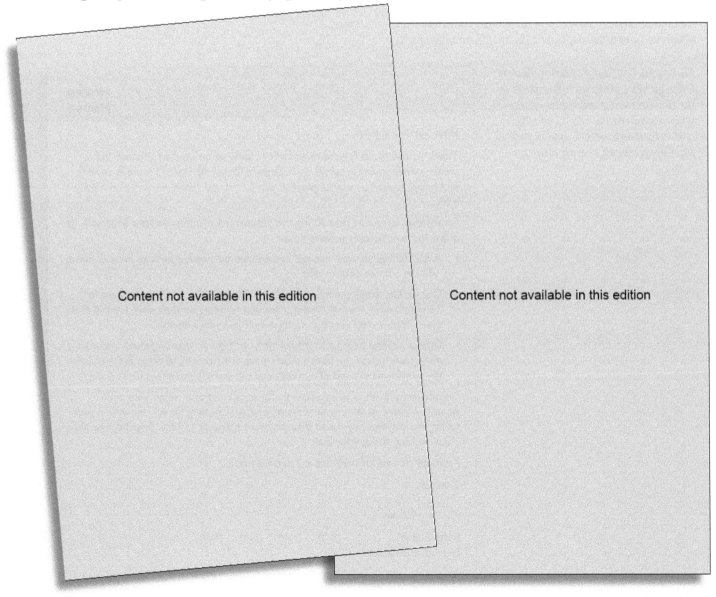

Content not available in this edition

CORRESPONDENCE, PRINTED COMMUNICATIONS THAT SUPPORT STEWARDSHIP EFFORTS

Donor Impact Reports Help Illustrate How Gifts Make a Positive Difference

Donor relations staff at The University of Kansas Hospital (Kansas City, KS) create donor impact reports as a tool to communicate to donors how their gift has made a positive difference in the area or program to which it was designated.

"Impact reports communicate our stewardship of their gift and keep donors engaged in future developments of the institution," says Andrea Villasi, program coordinator of donor relations for hospital fund development. "Frequent, personalized communication with your donors demonstrates the institution's and the fundraiser's responsibility to the donor. Communications like these strengthen the relationship with the donor."

Reports are customized to fit the size and scope of the gift and donor's personality, Villasi says. They are usually two to three pages long and include financial information, information on how the gift was used and plans for the remainder of the gift.

"Since our institution is a hospital, we also include stories about how our physicians, nurses and other staff have touched patients' lives," she says. "Adding color, photos and different fonts make the reports interesting and enticing to the donor."

While any level donor may receive a report, Villasi says because the documents are so personal and detailed, they are usually reserved for major donors, those under cultivation or those with whom the hospital has a special relationship.

Reports are generally sent one year after a gift is made, she says. "Any less than that and we might not have enough data to warrant a comprehensive report. Any more than 18 months might make a statement to the donor that we have forgotten about them, or that we aren't utilizing their gift as expected."

The number of reports donors receive depends on their relationship with the hospital, gift lifespan and if the donor has capacity or intention to give again. Many donors receive an impact report once a year until the fund is depleted or the purpose of the gift has been fulfilled.

For organizations considering using donor impact reports as a stewardship tool, Villasi offers this advice:

"Know your donors and customize their reports to fit their personalities. If they are business savvy and are driven to give as an investment in their community, for example, the report should focus more on the financial outcomes of their gift. If the donor was compelled to give because of an emotional experience, touching stories of how their gift has helped others will mean more to them than the amount of investment income that their gift has accrued in the last year."

Source: Andrea Villasi, Program Coordinator, Donor Relations, Hospital Fund Development, The University of Kansas Hospital, Westwood, KS. Phone (913) 588-1433. E-mail: avillasi@kumc.edu

This sample donor impact report illustrates how donor relations staff at The University of Kansas Hospital (Kansas City, KS) personalize information to specific donors.

Content not available in this edition

Keep Long-distance Donors Up-to-date On Key Issues

Out of sight, out of mind. It's easy to lose track of the number of communications you've had with donors whose geographic locations prevent you from seeing them on a regular basis. Before you know it, it's time to make a visit to solicit another gift, and you realize minimal time has been devoted to cultivation and stewardship moves that are so important in securing that repeat and, hopefully, increased gift.

To stay in touch with your long distance donors on a more regular basis, provide them with a personalized letter at least quarterly if not monthly. In drafting those regularly sent letters, keep the following points in mind:

- While some of the messages in those letters can be standardized, be sure that portions of each letter are more personal in nature. Include messages that may tie back to issues discussed in your last face-to-face meeting with the donor or discuss the impact their gift is having on your organization and those you serve. But whatever the message, make it personal to them and your relationship to them.

- Select words that make your letter more conversational in style and not contrived. Picture sitting in the living room of one of your donors, visiting with them, as you craft your letter.

- Look back on events that have taken place at your organization since the last letter was sent. What accomplishments have taken place for which you are most proud? What key issues are facing your organization that others would want to know? Summarize those points — which can be standardized — in the body of your letter.

At right is a sample letter to which you can refer in developing letters of your own as regular updates for your long-distance donors. Note how the first two paragraphs and concluding paragraph are highly personalized, with the key points being standardized as a template that would be included in letters being sent to multiple long-distance donors.

The sender also enclosed a copy of the local newspaper as an added touch.

Sample fictitious letter designed to illustrate regular communication with long-distance donors.

THE MUSEUM OF
MORGAN COUNTY

July 15, 2010

Dear John and Betty:

It's hard to believe nearly seven months have passed since I was in your home during my trip to Los Angeles. I think about you and your skills at selecting — and knowing when to sell — stocks, every time I turn to The Financial News Network. You certainly have "the touch."

I know you also take a keen interest at what is happening back here in Albia, Nebraska — this being your childhood home. And we're so grateful for your interest in and commitment to our museum as well. That's why I like to update you, from time to time, on some key points I believe you'll find of interest.

Since I last wrote to you in April:

- We have taken the first steps in outlining a new strategic plan, the results of which we hope will bring greater regional attention to our museum and attract significantly greater numbers of visitors. In addition to local involvement from community leaders and donors, we intend to seek the opinions of some of our long-distance patrons — including yourselves — at some future point. To be continued.

- We recently acquired a phenomenal treasure of Native American artifacts from a site 35 miles from here that will no doubt draw regional, and perhaps, national attention. Although there could be some controversy regarding the project, we're confident these artifacts will provide a lasting tribute to the Native American culture of this region.

- We added three new and outstanding board members to our museum at our last board meeting: Philanthropist Alan Grimshaw of Newkirk, Marc Wetlestein of Omaha, Chairman of Landsco, and Susan Hartmann, M.D., of Wichita, Kansas. We are indeed fortunate to have these individuals among our illustrious Board of Directors.

As you can imagine, I will be telling you more about the first two issues mentioned as they continue to unfold. This is an exciting time for the museum, and we are deeply grateful to have both of you so closely involved with and committed to our work here.

Please give my regards to your son, Tom, and please feel free to call me at any time.

Most sincerely,

Robert F. Peterson
Executive Director

P.S. I have included the most recent issue of *The Albia Times* for you. I know you enjoy reading about what's happening in your hometown.

The Museum of Morgan County • PO Box 322 • Albia, NE 68909 • Phone 402.333.0404

Letters of Apology Go With the Territory

You are in the midst of a major donor appreciation banquet and suddenly discover, while browsing the list of donors in the printed program, that the spouse of a major donor does not have her name included.

When it's obvious that someone at your end has made a big mistake — and sometimes when it's not so obvious — it's important to take immediate action to make things right and quell any ill feelings a donor might be experiencing. The best action is a face-to-face apology. But even when that's possible, a follow-up written letter of apology is in order.

Your letter of apology should possess these key characteristics:

1. **It need not be lengthy.** People don't want a lengthy explanation of why something went wrong. Nor do they want an apology repeated over and over again. Keep your message brief and to the point.

2. **Your letter should be genuine.** Speak from your heart. Write in a conversational tone as though you were visiting face-to-face.

3. **It should not be filled with excuses, but it should address why such a mistake occurred.** If a name was inadvertently omitted, say why. And if you have absolutely no reason why it happened, tell the donor just that.

4. **The message should pledge that such a mistake will not occur again.** Be courageous enough to pledge that such a mistake won't happen again. Doing so will make you and your staff more vigilant in the future.

Shown to the right is a sample apology letter.

Dear Betty:

On behalf of (Name of Organization), I want to again apologize for our failure to include your name along with your husband, John, in our Donor Appreciation Banquet program. I deeply regret this error on our part.

In spite of our efforts to proofread the program prior to its printing — three members of our staff reviewed the list — we still goofed up in a big way.

To ensure that this will never happen again, we have made multiple notes — in your file and in our banquet evaluation for next year's event. We have also double-checked the soon-to-be-printed Annual Report to be sure your name is listed correctly in that document.

We are so very grateful for all that both you and John have done for our institution and those we serve. Please accept our sincere apologies.

Respectfully,

Thomas McMann
Director of Development

Stewardship Tip

■ Contact or send a personal note to each annual contributor of $1,000 or more six months after his/her last gift so the contributor is being reminded — six months prior to the next ask — of how important his/her support is to your organization and those you serve. Make note of this strategy in your annual stewardship plan.

Stewardship Essentials: The Donor Relations Guide.
Edited by Scott C. Stevenson.
© 2011 Stevenson, Inc. Published 2011 by Stevenson, Inc.

Stewardship Essentials: The Donor Relations Guide

WEBSITE STEWARDSHIP STRATEGIES

These days, even your website can provide a valuable source of stewardship assistance by educating donors, keeping them informed, recognizing their generosity, engaging them and more.

Show Donors the Money (and Where It Goes)

Anything you can do to show donors how their gifts make a difference will increase donors' confidence and make them more likely to give in the future.

Colleen Townsley Brinkmann, chief marketing officer, North Texas Food Bank (Dallas, TX), says a website illustration helps show donors where their food and financial donations go.

Visitors to the organization's website (www.ntfb.org) simply click on "Donate," then "Food" to find the link to the graphic chart, "Follow Your Donation."

Shown below, the graphic illustrates how food donations benefit 917 feeding and education programs in a 13-county area.

The page also helps educate donors and others about the work of the food pantry, which Townsley Brinkmann says is paramount: "We were having trouble getting people to understand we're not a cozy, little food pantry — we're a distribution agency. (And) by helping us you are helping tens of thousands of people."

The page averages 754 hits per month.

Source: Colleen Townsley Brinkmann, Chief Marketing Officer; Mark Armstrong, Senior Manager-Internet and New Media, North Texas Food Bank, Dallas, TX. Phone (214) 347-9594.

Website Offers Giving Tools

Visitors to the North Texas Food Bank (Dallas, TX) website find several tools to encourage gifts. For example, starting at the home page (www.ntfb.org), visitors can:

Learn how to start an actual or virtual canned food drive —
Click "Donate," "Food," and select "Conduct a Canned or Virtual Food Drive" in pop-up menu to register and receive tips for gathering food or cash gifts.

See inside the food bank — Select "About Us" and "Virtual Tour."

Share the passion — Click "Media Room" and "Video Features" for online videos explaining food bank programs and how they help combat hunger in North Texas.

This online illustration shows North Texas Food Bank donors how their gifts help others.

Content not available in this edition

Personalized Websites Bring Smiles to Donors, Children in Need

The more closely a person relates to an organization's mission, the more motivated he or she is to donate money to it and ask others to donate, too.

C. Eric Overman, director of online and interactive, Operation Smile (Norfolk, VA), says its OneSmile program definitely makes their mission real and relatable for those donors who use it. OneSmile allows donors to easily set up their own Web page to raise funds to cover the cost of life-changing surgery for one child.

The ability to make a personal page provided the perfect way to connect supporters to the cause online, Overman says.

"In a few easy steps, online donors can build their own Web page, tell their story and invite friends to join in. Just like with social media, it is a friend asking you to support us, not us asking you for money," he says, adding: "Since we launched (the personal page option in 2007), almost 400 pages have been set up, raising nearly $150,000."

When considering such a project, Overman says to make sure you have the technology necessary to run the program and that the technology fully integrates into your other systems.

Also, he says, be aware of the costs, which can vary greatly depending on several factors, including your current Web and e-mail platforms and in-house technology resources.

Finally, have a plan to market the opportunity to current and prospective donors.

"Just because you build it doesn't mean they will come," he says. "You will still need to promote the site and integrate custom campaigns into the major events and marketing campaigns running across your organization."

Source: C. Eric Overman, Director of Online and Interactive, Operation Smile, Norfolk, VA. Phone (757) 321-3252. E-mail: eoverman@operationsmile.org

Video Lets Donors Meet the People Their Gifts Help

As a donor, what would it mean to you to be able to directly see the faces of the people you have helped?

Zach Pretzer, associate director, Oberlin Alumni Fund, Oberlin College (Oberlin, OH) says a video created by Oberlin to honor and thank the college's generous scholarship donors does just that.

The nine-minute video is featured on the college's website (www.oberlin.edu/giving/scholarshipvideo/). It offers testimonials from those who have received scholarships to Oberlin as well as those who have made donations in support of Oberlin's scholarship programs.

Scholarship recipients also share reasons specific to their own situations about why scholarship gifts are so important.

Sophisticated and creative editing adds the final polish to the piece.

Pretzer says the video is just one example of the way Oberlin makes stewardship a priority. "We excel in strengthening relationships with donors by honoring those who invest in Oberlin and help serve the needs of our donors through scholarship reporting, recognition and events."

Source: Zachary Pretzer, Associate Director, Oberlin Alumni Fund, Oberlin College, Oberlin, OH. Phone (440) 775-5537. E-mail: zach.pretzer@oberlin.edu

What Donors Expect From Your Website

Donors have certain expectations when visiting your website, says Michel Hudson, owner of 501(c)onsulting (Round Rock, TX): "Donors want to feel connected to your organization and as though they are part of your family. They also want to know that you have similar outlooks and objectives to theirs."

To fulfill those donor expectations, says Hudson:

- **Have compelling website copy.** Your text needs to compel them to donate, participate in a call to action and/or read more about your organization. It should inform people about your cause, what you are doing and how they can help.
- **Tell them where the money goes.** This makes them feel confident about your cause.
- **Share your research and any results, insights or successes.** People want to know more about what interests them and that's why they are coming to your site.
- **Make it easy and secure for visitors to make donations.** You want to limit the number of steps it takes to get to the donation.
- **Include a prominent and well-stated privacy policy.**
- **Make sure website content is fresh.** This gives donors confidence in your organization. "Be aware that search engine optimization is based on freshness," Hudson notes. "The more your content changes, the higher rankings you will get with search engines. But don't change things just for change — make it meaningful."

Source: Michel Hudson, Owner, 501(c)onsulting, Round Rock, TX. Phone (512) 565-0142. E-mail: mhudson@501consulting.com

Stewardship Essentials: The Donor Relations Guide

FITTING EXAMPLES OF STEWARDSHIP IN ACTION

What are you doing in the way of stewardship that's unique to your organization? Following are some examples of what other nonprofits are doing to steward their donors and demonstrate, in multiple ways, the impact of their generosity.

Elm Tree Society Thanks, Stewards Donors

Honor rolls, luncheons and gifts are just a few of the ways to thank and steward donors.

Staff with Scripps College (Claremont, CA) created a donor recognition society that uses those three methods and more. Currently some 300 members strong, the Elm Tree Society began in the early 1990s to honor and highlight planned giving donors and as a way for the college to show its appreciation to donors through elite events and gifts.

Allyson Simpson, director of planned giving, shares the details of the society:

What are the criteria to belong to the Elm Tree Society?

"A person must have made a life-income gift (e.g., charitable gift annuity, charitable remainder trust, etc.) or have communicated a testamentary bequest intention, including the designation of the college as the beneficiary of a life insurance policy, commercial annuity or a retirement plan, such as an IRA, 401(k) or 403(b) plan."

What does the college do with the society?

"We use the society to steward existing donors, thank and cultivate them for additional planned gifts. It has an aura of specialness about it, especially with respect to the appreciation gifts we give members, which usually bear the special society logo. This specialness also serves as an attraction for prospects we are cultivating as new planned giving donors."

What does the college do for members of the society?

"First, we feature the members prominently in the annual Honor Roll of Donors. Second, we hold at least two lunch/program events a year on campus and one or more lunch events in off-campus locations where we have a critical mass geographically of members. Usually the president of the college welcomes and thanks those in attendance at the on-campus events. Third, once a year... we present all members (in person or by mail if they cannot attend the lunch event) with a recognition gift that identifies them as society members."

Why is this society successful?

"We engage in constant, year-round stewardship and appreciation. Our members come to anticipate the events and the gifts, and seem to really enjoy both and feel good about what they have done for the future of the college."

What challenges do you face with this society? How are you overcoming them?

"Planning and executing the events and staying in touch with members who live out of the area. Because the membership is predominantly elderly, sometimes our attendance is lower than we'd like. It's difficult for some of our more elderly constituents to get to campus or the event site. We try to schedule lunch events in conjunction with other programs on campus so there will be other persons coming to campus who might be able to drive the more elderly members who do not drive anymore. We also try to match people up geographically so they can come together.... When we send gifts to out-of-area members who can't make it to campus, we always send a warm letter thanking them again for their thoughtful gift and reminding them how important they are to the future of the college."

What advice do you have for organizations interested in creating a similar society?

- "Select a name that means something to the constituent body, since planned giving is all about legacy, emotional attachment and ultimate gifts. Our name comes from the Elm Tree Lawn on campus where every commencement is held. Just a picture of the lawn with its canopy of elm trees evokes memories and a sense of timelessness.

- "Publicize the society to existing planned giving donors and to likely planned giving prospects.

- "Steward, steward, steward on a consistent basis and show appreciation in important and visible, but relatively inexpensive, ways. We produce official membership certificates on a desktop computer that are signed by the college president. I try to choose recognition gifts that are useful for older persons (e.g., luggage tag, pocket or purse notebook, key ring with light, umbrella) and are inexpensive per unit, but still very classy, in the college's colors with the Elm Tree Society logo prominently displayed."

Source: Allyson Simpson, Director of Planned Giving, Scripps College, Claremont, CA. Phone (909) 621-8400.
E-mail: allyson.simpson@scrippscollege.edu

Organization Combines Donor, Volunteer Recognition Events

Staff with the American Red Cross of the Quad Cities Area (Moline, IL) took a chance combining the organization's volunteer and donor recognition events to create a single event that enjoyed overwhelming success.

"Everyone was delighted with the event and all indicated that it was a great way for both volunteers and donors to feel more like one unit," says Patti Franklin, director of public support. "We will continue to do a combined event in the future, and I would encourage other organizations to plan one. Not only is it cost effective, but it gives both donors and volunteers another perspective on the organization that they already support, and it deepens the relationship that each has with the organizational mission."

The move to combine the two events came at the suggestion of a volunteer as the planned giving committee was trying to set a date for the donor recognition event.

"In the discussion, everyone realized that it would save money and help donors and volunteers understand more deeply how both types of gifts ensure the stability of the organization," Franklin says. "We were able to save substantially by combining the events. Plus, it was a wonderful educational opportunity for both donors and volunteers."

The Red Cross chapter invited members of its Legacy Society (planned gift donors) and Clara Barton Society (those making an annual gift of $1,000 or more), as well as all volunteers. The recognition event, which ran from 5 to 7 p.m., included heavy hors d'oeuvres, coffee, punch and a cash bar.

The program highlighted each of the groups in attendance:

✓ Volunteers with increments of five years of service received service pins. Additionally, a volunteer shared his reasons for volunteering as well as his experiences with the hurricane relief efforts.

✓ Members of the Clara Barton Society received pins and attendees learned about the society.

✓ Attendees learned the qualifications to be members of the Legacy Society as current members came forward.

Following the event, Franklin says volunteers and staff members contacted 53 of the 140 attendees for feedback.

From the volunteer perspective, she says: "A wider Red Cross audience saw, heard and appreciated what they spend many hours doing each year. One volunteer remarked that he was amazed to see how many volunteers work in the other programs and services at the Red Cross. Another said that he learned how big our Red Cross chapter is and how well it is supported financially."

"We were able to save substantially by combining the events. Plus, it was a wonderful educational opportunity for both donors and volunteers."

On the flip side, Franklin says: "Donors had the opportunity to talk informally to volunteers about what they do and heard about their passion for the work they donate to the community through Red Cross. Some donors have inquired about volunteering since the event. One donor indicated that, 'it added a lot for donors to see what is going on at Red Cross.' Two said that the event spoke to how important volunteers are to Red Cross that they continue to give their time for more than 60 years."

Another benefit of the combined event has been an increase in the attendance at Red Cross 101 sessions, one-hour meetings to learn more about the organization.

"We've held these Red Cross 101 programs for two years but struggled to get people to attend," Franklin says. "After the recognition event, 21 of the 53 volunteers and donors we called scheduled a time to attend the program during the next three months" and wanted to know the schedule for the next year."

Although it is still too early to see an increase in donations or in donors, Franklin is optimistic, as feedback has been so positive. She says the chapter is planning an upcoming ask that involves multi-year financial pledges. Many of those asked will be those cultivated through the combined recognition event and the Red Cross 101 sessions.

Source: Patti Franklin, Director of Public Support, American Red Cross of the Quad Cities Area, Moline, IL. Phone (309) 743-2166. E-mail: franklinp@usa.redcross.org

Make Sure Smaller Donors Know Their Donations Matter

Jamie Leszczynski, associate director of annual giving, The Fund for Oswego (Oswego, NY) is hoping to strike gold with the department's most recent direct mail appeal to benefit the State University at New York (SUNY) Oswego.

The mailing, sent to 7,774 Graduates of the Last Decade (GOLD), is intended to show how even the small donations are important and add up.

Leszczynski says the idea came from the fundraising committee of a leadership council created specifically to target this group of alumni. The committee reviewed marketing pieces from the last several years and compiled suggestions and recommendations.

The committee wanted something short and simple, all in one piece, she says. Planners chose $25 as the target donation to keep it affordable for everyone.

The marketing piece, shown below, lets donors know that "if every graduate from Oswego in the past 10 years gave a gift of $25 this year, the college could support students with an additional $380,925."

Leszczynski says feedback for the piece has been positive, with 42 percent of gifts to date coming from first-time donors. Thirty-eight percent of the donors responding to the piece gave more than the suggested $25, including three who gave $100 each.

She notes that the project has reaped a valuable lesson for the fund's staff: "Get alumni involved with reviewing your pieces and have them assist with the text. They know what they want to see and what works for them."

Source: Jamie Stack Leszczynski, Associate Director of Annual Giving, The Fund for Oswego, SUNY Oswego, Oswego, NY. Phone (315) 312-3121. E-mail: leszczyn@oswego.edu

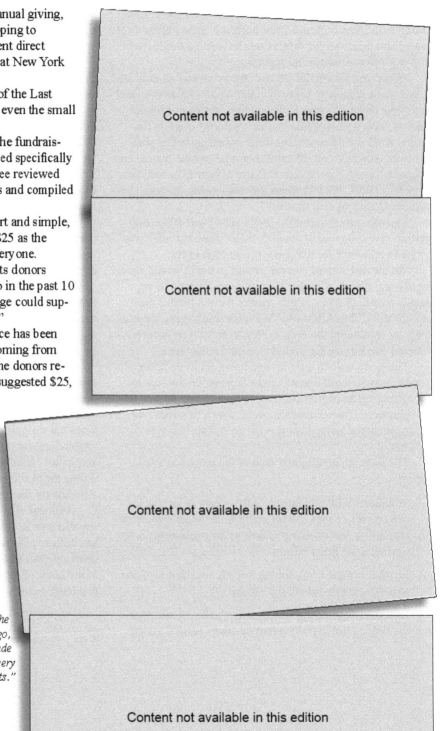

Direct mail pieces from a campaign for The Fund for Oswego, SUNY Oswego (Oswego, NY) target graduates from the last decade with an ask of just $25, emphasizing "every gift counts."

Institute's Program Reconnects Donors, Forges Friendships

If a major donor has faith in the overall excellence of an institution, he or she is much more likely to feel comfortable becoming a long-term investor in that institution. This is the thought behind the Pitt Institute at the University of Pittsburgh (Pittsburgh, PA), a program that offers intellectually appropriate cultivation events for a major gift officer's portfolio.

Since it was organized in 2008, the institute has hosted 10 on-campus events that have drawn more than 600 alumni. One recent event featured one of the university's anthropology professors offering an up-close look at his life-sized reconstructions of George Washington, based on three years of forensic research and featured in the *Washington Post* and on The History Channel.

The events, and the unique opportunities they offer, help feed major gift solicitation efforts, says David Dalessandro, associate vice chancellor of university development.

"It is one thing for the chancellor to say, 'We are great because of such-and-such accomplishment,' and quite another for a 70-year-old alumni to see Saturn through a century-old telescope," Dalessandro says. "We believe that any time we gather prospects and excite them about the university's excellence, it helps our efforts."

The institute does not focus on a specific school or program. "Simply put, the mission of the institute is to give donors an appreciation of the larger university mission: the creation and preservation of knowledge," he says. "A secondary goal is to make local alumni feel that the Pitt campus welcomes their continued presence as adult learners."

To create invitation lists to the exclusive events, the Pitt Institute maintains an alumni donor list of about 3,000 names of persons who graduated before 1970. Invitations are sent by traditional mail, with e-mail and the institute's website playing an important part in the process, too. Major gift officers also extend personal invitations to their prospects.

Fuel Donor Interaction With Mini Profiles

At your next special event, arm development staff with mini profiles of each guest — condensed versions of the extensive files you keep on each donor — so conversational material is readily available, says Liz Cooper, director of constituent relations, University of Pittsburgh (Pittsburgh, PA). Include in the mini profiles:

- ✓ Guest's name/spouse's name.
- ✓ Guest's photo, if available.
- ✓ Employment information.
- ✓ College name/degree/year of graduation.
- ✓ Giving history.
- ✓ Affiliations (for example, member, African American Alumni Council).
- ✓ Other (in the university's case, this might be something like, "parent of Grace Lu, Class of 2014").

Source: Liz B. Cooper, Director of Constituent Relations, University of Pittsburgh, Pittsburgh, PA.

Another key step is compiling profiles of all those attending, says Dalessandro (see box). "Our staff attempts to engage everyone in a personal conversation at the event and new prospects are visited."

He notes that to date, about 60 percent of institute attendees are repeats, many of whom make major gifts.

Source: David Dalessandro, Associate Vice Chancellor for University Development, Pitt Institute, Pittsburgh, PA. Phone (412) 624-8239. E-mail: ddaavid@pitt.edu. Website: www.giveto.pitt.edu

College Pins Annual Fund on Leadership Donors

Annual fund gifts are critical to ongoing success of Macalester College (St. Paul, MN). So development staff make a concentrated effort to steward and cultivate leadership-level donors through three societies. Those donors' combined gifts accounted for about $2.5 million of the total $3.1 million raised by the fund last fiscal year.

Continued and varied recognition helps celebrate these donors and encourage others to join them, says Elissa Chaffee, annual fund director.

Depending on gift size, donors become members of the Grand Society ($1,000-$4,999), Tartan Society ($5,000-$9,999) or the Highland Society ($10,000 and up). All society donors receive special recognition in publications, personal correspondence from the college president and invitations to special events.

All society donors also receive the Macalester Tartan shield pin — a favorite of leadership donors, Chaffee says, adding: "Members are encouraged to wear them at college events and are quick to tell us if they need a replacement pin."

The different giving levels, Chaffee says, offer the ability to attract and retain higher-level annual fund donors, provide an incentive for donors to move up to the next society and create a community within the annual fund through the events and special recognition.

Source: Elissa Chaffee, Director of the Annual Fund, Macalester College, St. Paul, MN. Phone (651) 696-6099. E-mail: echaffee@macalester.edu

Giving Society Celebrates Consistent Donor Support

At Agnes Scott College (Decatur, GA), gift size takes a back seat to donor loyalty when it comes to recognition.

The college's Fideles Society recognizes donor loyalty without regard to the amount of giving, emphasizing that every gift counts, says Joanne Davis, director of the annual fund. College officials, Davis says, were looking for an incentive to encourage donors to give each year, "and we were also looking for a way to recognize donors no matter what size their gift, knowing that not everyone can make large gifts."

Thus, the Fideles Society was born.

Today, at just three years of age, the society boasts more than 3,000 members.

Here's how the program works:

Donors who give to the annual fund for three consecutive years become members of the Fideles Society, regardless of the amount of those gifts. Members receive a car decal with the Fideles Society logo and have an "F" by their name in the annual report.

Members receive a spring mailing encouraging them to give to maintain their membership. Phonathon callers also have a record of the alumna's giving and are able to remind society members that a gift will maintain their membership.

College officials are also considering designing a new decal to celebrate five-year members of the society.

Benefits to the college are obvious, she says. "It gives us a strong nucleus of donors we can depend on year after year. For the past seven years our alumnae participation has averaged between 42 and 47 percent."

Before embarking on a similar project, Davis recommends, make sure giving records are accurate and talk to other charities with similar recognition programs.

Source: Joanne Davis, Director of the Annual Fund, Agnes Scott College, Decatur, GA. Phone (404) 471-5343.
E-mail: jadavis@agnesscott.edu

Donor Recognition Idea

Looking for a creative way to share the impact of a major gift with the donor who made it all happen? LaShon Anthony, small business consultant with visuals4u (Chicago, IL), shares an out-of-this-world method: Name a star after the donor.

This opportunity is available through the International Star Registry (Ingleside, IL). Learn more at http://starregistry.com.

Source: LaShon Anthony, Small Business Consultant, visuals4u, Chicago, IL. E-mail: info@visuals4u.com.
Website: http://visuals4u.com